A Coursebook for Leaders of Adults

THE PARABLES
OF JESUS

by Eugene S. Wehrli

UNITED CHURCH PRESS

Boston Philadelphia

OTHER MATERIALS FOR THIS COURSE:

Exploring the Parables,
a resource book for
adult study groups
Five Parables of Jesus,
a sound-color filmstrip that
visualizes the parables
of "The Sower,"
"The Good Samaritan,"
"The Lost Sheep,"
""The Prodigal Son,"
and "The Talents."

This book is part of the
United Church Curriculum,
prepared and published by the
Division of Christian Education and the
Division of Publication
of the United Church Board
for Homeland Ministries.

Library of Congress
Catalog Card No. 63-17255

Contents

Introduction

THE SCOPE OF THE COURSE

A complete course in itself, *The Parables of Jesus* is also part of a larger plan: the United Church Curriculum. It is prepared as the course for adults in a semester in which the theme that unifies the work of all age levels is "Growing as a Christian." For many Sunday morning church school classes this will mean that they will be using the course during the five-month semester of the United Church Curriculum from September 1963 through January 1964. Other church school classes may be using this course at a later date, as an elective, or at a meeting time other than Sunday mornings. Still other adult study groups may be using the course for Sunday evening or week-night sessions, in leadership training schools, on weekend retreats, or as program resource material for monthly meetings of a church organization for adults.

Whenever and in whatever circumstances you are using this course, you will be devoting yourselves to an intensive study of the parables of Jesus. Since it is impossible to know the precise meaning and specific use of a given parable without being familiar with the manner in which the church understood it, applied it, and passed it on, it will be inevitable that you will need to set the parables in their context. In a sense the parables will lead you into the total mission and message of Jesus Christ—so important are they to his teaching and to his role as the son of God.

A study of the parables of Jesus inevitably leads us to the meaning of our Christian growth and our living together. What kind of a person does God want me to be? What do the parables of Jesus mean? The implication of the parables for these questions can be the topic of group discussions. Once the meaning of the parable is established the members of the group can contribute some of the implications for life. The group leader must try to provide situations in which such discovery can take place. As the implications for life are shared, the insight of each member is widened by seeing the parable taking on relevance for actual situations and for his growth as a Christian. We cannot discern the meaning of the parables without finding material relevant to how we live and to the purpose for which we are here.

THE PURPOSE OF THE COURSE

The primary purpose of this course is to understand the words of Jesus and the ways of God's working as they are made known in the parables. We must learn how to read a parable to gain the meaning which Jesus gave. Although it may have many implications or applications, each parable has one and only one central meaning. To uncover it, close study of the parable is essential. Great care must be exercised in giving a parable implications or applications based on its one central meaning. But once we have studied the parable and arrived at some comprehension of what the parable was meant to say we should apply it to our lives. The early church did this with the parables, applying them to the various situations which its members faced. Now it is our responsibility to relate their meanings to our situation.

THE APPROACH OF THE COURSE

The resource book is designed to give as clear an interpretation of the parables of Jesus as is possible. It is felt that the reader will be able to understand the discussion in the resource book only if he has the Bible in front of him and the parts of the parable in mind. He will have to follow the ideas presented in the resource book and in the parable itself, and either discover them also for himself or test them by the very wording of the parable. The resource book and the Bible are to be *studied*, not merely read.

When asked a question in Bible study, most people will not answer on the basis of a close examination of the biblical text, but out of an inherited conception of the Christian faith—whether or not this is what the Bible says in a specific passage. It is not important in this course for the leader to know everything, but it is important that he continually keep the group conscious of what the Bible says, stresses, and emphasizes. For example, if asking the meaning of the parable of the lost sheep, one is likely to hear that the parable stresses the quality of love that is concerned for every person without exception. But is this really what the parable stresses? Such ideas are only tested by looking long and hard at the biblical text and by answering such questions as: What is the main point of the parable as told? To whom is the parable addressed and for what purpose? When such questions have been dealt with seriously the group is in a position to decide the validity of the original statement. It takes some serious study and not off-the-cuff remarks to determine whether the parable of the sower really illustrates that not all people respond favorably to the message proclaimed by Jesus. Is this really what the parable was meant to say? Or is it at best a by-product of the parable? It takes thorough study of the biblical text to answer such questions.

The resource book is to be used as an aid to such study, and you as the leader have the responsibility of asking the searching questions that drive people back to the text of the Bible in order to test the validity of the statements that men often make on the basis of general opinion rather than on study of the actual words of the Bible.

Such study as we have been discussing should be engaged in by the group both at home and in the group experience. Reminding people to deal with the text and not in generalities might have to be accomplished in the group session first before members can satisfactorily test their own answers at home. Yet, in order to study the word of God in such a way that it speaks to us, it is necessary to expect such rigorous thinking from members outside as well as during the group session. This will have value for the individual's study in preparation for forthcoming sessions, or for gathering materials, or for discovering incidents to which the parable is applicable.

In addition to this careful reading and encounter with the text, Bible study can be made fruitful by asking the group to imagine their reaction if they had been in the audience to which the parable was originally addressed. If the Pharisees were the target, let them imagine how the Pharisees would feel and react; if the parable is directed to the multitude of the common people, let them imagine how the common people would respond. To do this effectively, let someone gather data on who the Pharisees were and how they looked at things, or what were the characteristic attitudes held toward religion by the multitude.

The final stage of study is for the group to put themselves in the places of modern groups of people and attempt to feel how they would respond to the parable. How would a group of businessmen react to a given story? Professional men? Theologians? Labor? The multitude? What feelings would the parable raise? Let the group try to feel themselves into the situation of certain groups and individuals and have them talk back to the parable, raising objections that are pertinent from the point of view of the particular individuals they represent. When this talk-back is gathered and recorded it can become the basis of a good discussion.

Finally let the group express their own frank reactions and objections to the message of the parable so that a real encounter and discussion can take place where the parable and our point of view conflict most. Let the group explore whether the parables go against the way that we have to live in our twentieth century society. Encourage the members of the group to be themselves and to challenge the parable at points where they do not see eye-to-eye, just as they would argue with their next-door neighbor. Only in such a way can the word of God get at our deepest emotions and most fundamental ideas.

THE RESOURCE BOOK, *EXPLORING THE PARABLES*

The resource book is organized according to the number of chapters that the subject warrants rather than the number of sessions your group plans to have. Such an organization of the resource book is designed to give the subject the balanced treatment that its material demands. Things do not have to be juggled to fit an arbitrary number of sessions.

It is very important for you to explain the nature of the resource book to your group, especially if they have been accustomed to a week-by-week book. Be sure to help them to understand that this is a paperback reading book of the kind they would buy in a bookstore. As such it is designed to be read in its entirety as early in the course as possible.

The chapter headings in the resource book indicate the general subject areas of the parables. Because of their broad spectrum they are not easily placed in sharply defined categories, and they could very often be placed under other headings than the one given. The grouping points out certain aspects of significance in the parables but often by-passes others which a different scheme of organization might point out. At other times it will be evident that two seemingly different parables actually have the same point and are grouped together as twin parables.

Chapters one, two, and three are introductory chapters. They deal with the nature of parables and with the setting of the parables or the occasions for which they were told or repeated. As Jesus told the parables and as the early church repeated them, the parables were applied to the problems of the day. Several applications are often given for the same parable, because it is applied to different situations. The third chapter seeks to explore these facts and to discover how the meaning relates to the various problems faced by the men who retold the parables. The final chapter of the resource book, chapter ten, deals with the place of Jesus in the message of the parables. Not only does the teaching of several parables relate to Jesus' position, but all of them in their method and telling relate to the broad dimensions of this question.

THIS COURSEBOOK, *THE PARABLES OF JESUS*

The book you are now reading is called the coursebook. Except for the introductory unit, this course is organized by grouping the parables by subject matter or by their main emphases. As is shown by the outline of the units on page 11, Unit II is concerned with the *Parables of the Kingdom,* Unit III deals with *Disciples of the Kingdom,* and Unit IV considers *The Ways of God with Man.*

Unit numbers are given in roman numerals and session numbers in arabic numerals. For example, I–3 indicates session three of unit one; IV–3 means session three of unit four. The pages of this coursebook are numbered consecutively from 1 to 128 at the top of the page. The numbers at the bottom are unit and session numbers.

The numbering of the sessions is done by unit and session rather than by session alone because this gives greater flexibility to the use of this course. Many groups that are using this course in relatively short-term study groups, for example, will find it desirable to use only unit I and one of the other three units. Such numbering makes such use possible. It also helps us to think and to work in terms of units. This becomes an aid in remembering the outline and the progression of the course.

The coursebook material is arranged for seventeen to twenty-one sessions. Some groups will want to use the course in more sessions; others will want to use it in short-term study (such as six- or ten-week courses). On occasion the resource book may be used at a retreat.

Four of the sessions are marked as optional. Groups that have less than seventeen sessions available may want to use Unit I in connection with only one or two of the other units. The first unit should be regarded as essential to any study, because it discusses the nature and purpose of the parables of Jesus.

It is also expected that most of the sessions will contain more biblical material than can profitably be discussed in the class session. Do not feel bound to discuss all passages or parables, but make the parables you do discuss a rich and rewarding experience. The rest can be left to the use of the resource book and home study. It is better to cover one or two parables thoroughly than to cover all superficially. If a few parables come alive through group sessions, and if the members of the group learn to study a parable for its central meaning, they will be able to deal with the other parables on their own. Comprehension is to be desired more than comprehensiveness.

THE FILMSTRIP, *FIVE PARABLES OF JESUS*

A sound–color filmstrip entitled *Five Parables of Jesus* has been prepared for use as part of the resource material for this course. It visualizes the parables of the sower, the good Samaritan, the lost sheep, the prodigal son, and the talents. The record contains the reading of the parables from the Bible, while the artist has applied his skills to the visual portrayal of what is being read.

This coursebook gives suggestions as to the sessions in which portions of the filmstrip might be used. It is suggested that you use the portion on the parable of the lost sheep as part of session I–3 (see page 41 of this course book); the parable of the talents in session III–3 (see page 86); the parable of the sower in session III–4 (see page 90); the parable of the good Samaritan in session III–7 (see page 102); and the parable of the prodigal son in session IV–1 (see page 114).

THE OUTLINE OF THE UNITS

The separate sessions of the course fall into certain natural groupings called units. They include:

UNIT I. THE NATURE AND USE OF PARABLES (3 OR 4 SESSIONS)

Here we endeavor to discover what a parable is and what we need to know and look for in order to interpret it properly.

UNIT II. PARABLES OF THE KINGDOM (5 OR 6 SESSIONS)

Here we study those parables that have the kingdom of God as their point of comparison.

The central theme in the teaching and action of Jesus, and hence the major subject of the parables, is the kingdom of God.

UNIT III. DISCIPLES OF THE KINGDOM (6 TO 8 SESSIONS)

The parables of the kingdom deal with God's action and purposes. Other parables are concerned with how men live in relation to this kingly rule of God. This unit falls into two parts. First, the demands that the kingdom lays on the disciples. Second, the new life of the disciple in the kingdom.

UNIT IV. THE WAY OF GOD WITH MAN (3 SESSIONS)

In the concluding unit the action of God is contrasted with the ways of man. The last question we raise is: What place does Jesus have in relation to the God of the kingdom and to his dealings with men?

The Outline of The Sessions

The following is the suggested plan of the sessions, listing the parables under the sessions in which they occur.

UNIT AND SESSION NUMBER	TOPIC	RESOURCE BOOK	BIBLICAL REFERENCE

UNIT I—THE NATURE AND USE OF PARABLES

I-1.	What is a Parable?	ch. 1-2	Mark 4: 26–29 The Seed Growing of Itself
I-2.	Learning to Read a Parable	ch. 1-2	Mark 4: 11–12
I-3.	The Life Situation	ch. 3	Matthew 18: 12–14; Luke 15: 3–7 The Lost Sheep Matthew 5: 23–26; Luke 12: 57–59 The Defendant
I-4.	The Context (optional)	ch. 3	Luke 13: 6–9 The Barren Fig Tree

UNIT II—PARABLES OF THE KINGDOM

II-1.	The Gift of the Kingdom	ch. 4	Matthew 20: 1–16 The Laborers in the Vineyard
II-2.	The Kingdom as an Invitation (optional)	ch. 4	Matthew 22: 1–11; Luke 14: 15–24 The Invitation to the Banquet (Wedding Feast) Matthew 22: 11–14 The Wedding Garment
II-3.	The Kingdom: Present and Coming	ch. 5	Matthew 13: 33; Luke 13: 20–21 The Leaven Matthew 13: 31–32; Mark 4: 30–32; Luke 13: 18–19 The Mustard Seed
II-4.	The Inclusiveness of the Kingdom	ch. 5	Matthew 13: 24–30 The Wheat and the Tares Matthew 13: 47–50 The Dragnet
II-5.	The Crisis of the Kingdom	ch. 6	Matthew 25: 1–13 The Ten Maidens
II-6.	The Judgment of the King	ch. 6	Matthew 25: 31–46 The Last Judgment

UNIT AND SESSION NUMBER	TOPIC	RESOURCE BOOK	REFERENCE BIBLICAL
			Luke 15: 8–10 The Lost Coin Luke 15: 11–32 The Prodigal Son
IV-2.	God's Miracles	ch. 9	Luke 16: 19–31 The Rich Man and Lazarus
IV-3.	Jesus in the Parables	ch. 10	Matthew 9: 16; Mark 2: 21; Luke 5: 36 The Unpatched Garment Matthew 19: 17; Mark 2: 22; Luke 5: 37–39 New Wine in Old Wineskins Matthew 12: 25–26; Mark 3: 23–26 Luke 11: 17–18 Satan Casting Out Satan Matthew 12: 29; Mark 3: 27; Luke 11: 21–22 The Strong Man

LISTINGS OF THE PARABLES

The appendix of the resource book gives two listings of the parables: an alphabetical listing with biblical references; and a biblical listing with parable names. (See pages 122–126 of the resource book, *Exploring the Parables.*

Any listing of the parables of Jesus is dependent upon one's definition of a parable. Lists vary because some biblical passages approach the dividing line that separates parables from other sayings. It is important to any study of the parables for the group to compare several listings of parables. In this way we learn that there is no one correct listing.

A major feature of this course is the suggestion that early in the course and at its conclusion the group study the appendix of the resource book by comparing it with other listings of the parables. In order to facilitate such comparative study we are including two other listings in this coursebook. One is from *The Interpreter's Bible* and the other from A. M. Hunter's *Interpreting the Bible*. These listings appear on pages 126–128 of this coursebook.

WORSHIP AND THE CLASS SESSION

A course planned to include discussion and contributions by members of the class cannot do justice to a great deal of material in a limited length of time. The assumption in these teaching plans is that there will be at least 45–50 minutes available for the study session. It is expected that adults will have their major experience of worship in the church service and that your sessions will need to provide very little opportunity for worship. The group session is designed to provide study, serious discussion, and activity. The members will want to attend the public worship of the congregation in order to praise God and know themselves as living under his rule.

On the other hand, meaningful worship, the recognition of God's dominion in a personally moving way, can come at any time—especially in a discussion of the teaching of Jesus, when suddenly that meaning becomes relevant to contemporary life. The leader should not be embarrassed at such moments, or hasten over them, but seek to enrich them. Meaningful worship may be encouraged by moments of silence, prayer, poetry, music or any other resource that the leader has available. At times the "thought for the leader" might seem appropriate for use during a moment of worship and reflection. Pictures and poems can also provide a brief but inspiring devotional focus.

At the conclusion of the discussion, the group period may be closed with prayer. If possible, let different members of the group offer the closing prayer each session. If members of the group are not accustomed to praying in public it will be courteous to ask them ahead of time until they get familiar with the practice. It is much better if you can spread this service around the group.

For opening the session the leader may offer prayer, or use a poem, picture, or thought. Singing a hymn together is not only a fine way to express our praise to God, but helps to give the group a feeling of unity and participation. If the group does not feel able to sing, the words of a hymn might be used and read in unison as a poem. Occasionally the opening thought in the session plans may be used as the opening thought for the group session.

ADDITIONAL RESOURCES

We have endeavored to make this a self-contained course. This means that we believe that you can have an interesting and productive study of the parables of Jesus by using nothing more than the Bible, the coursebook and the resource book. More and more, however, church libraries are making additional resources available to adult study groups. Since many of you will therefore want information as to how you can enhance your sessions even more through the use of additional resource materials, many sessions contain final sections that give suggestions for such possibilities. In most cases they are optional, additional resources that will enhance your session if you are able to make them available. If not, do not be concerned about them; if they are possibilities, they will contribute richly to the enhancing of your sessions. They can be used to answer questions or as the basis of reports.

Books on the parables can be listed in several categories. First, there are books that deal with the meaning of parables as Jesus told them. These books are concerned primarily with the meaning of the scriptural text. A very clear and easily understood book in this category is:

* Hunter, A. M., *Interpreting the Parables.*

More advanced books presenting the thought of scholars on the original meaning of the parables are:

Dodd, C. H., *The Parables of the Kingdom*
Oesterley, W. O. E., *The Gospel Parables in the Light of Their Jewish Background*
Smith, B. T. D., *The Parables of the Synoptic Gospels*

A second kind of book for getting at the meaning of parables is the commentary on the text of the scriptures which includes background information as well as comments on the meanings of key phrases.

A most helpful commentary which is most universally available is:

The Interpreter's Bible
Other helpful commentaries are:
   The Abingdon Bible Commentary
   The Torch Bible Commentaries
   The Laymen's Bible Commentary
   The Daily Study Bible by William Barclay provide insights into the meaning of passages and many resources for the application and relevance of the parables to contemporary life.

Books dealing with the contemporary relevance of the parables are difficult to find, but the sermons by Helmut Thielicke entitled *The Waiting Father* present excellent material for thought and further discussion on a number of the parables. Also, the expositions at the bottom of the page in *The Interpreter's Bible* provide application and relevance of the parable to life.

One of the most delightful yet incisive resources is the book of stories by Robert John Versteeg, *The Secret Life of the Good Samaritan.* Its stories "The Secret Life of the Good Samaritan," "The Prodigals," and "The Sheep" will greatly enhance both study and devotions. The low cost and the high quality of this book commend it to every group that uses this course.

Some modern expositions either do injustice to the central meaning of the original parable or focus their attention on an incidental feature of storytelling in the original parable. These expositions should not be used indiscriminately. Encourage the group to test the modern exposition, to make sure that it does justice to the central meaning of the biblical story and does not make a point of what was incidental in the story. The application and contemporary use of the parables should always be tested by serious study of the purpose of the parable. Statements in books endeavoring to point out relevance often strain so hard to find meaning that they lose sight of the point of view of the parable.

Some other books are referred to in the course of the session outlines to be used as resources. These books especially include the two collections by Cynthia Pearl Maus, *Christ and the Fine Arts* and *The Church and the*

Fine Arts. It is expected that these books and the ones referred to above marked with an asterisk (*) are likely to be the ones most frequently found in church libraries and most readily accessible to the class. References to a number of books and their use is made from time to time during the class session plans. It is not expected that you will have them all but that a few of them are available to you.

Another important resource is the *Manual for Adults* by Walter E. Dobler. This book, also a part of the United Church Curriculum, is the manual for leaders and administrators of adult study groups. It gives considerable help in understanding adults, in comprehending their interests and needs at various times during adulthood, in planning for your program for adults in the local church, and in preparing your rooms for teaching—with proper equipment, seating arrangements, and resource materials. It includes a helpful listing of addresses.

SUGGESTIONS FOR SESSIONS

Some of the sessions are covered in more detail than others. While suggestions are given, you will want to develop the session in your own way according to the make-up of your group. Ideas are given on the assumption that once you have begun to teach the course you will have developed patterns of working, and the group will contribute a great deal to the teaching and to the development of the sessions. There are more suggestions given for each session than can possibly be used. The extra material allows the leader some personal choice and provides for the variety of interest and composition of groups. Use this leeway to choose that which is most pertinent to your group.

Don't let your own personal feeling and experience limit the scope of your teaching. An effort has been made in the suggestions to provide for a number of kinds of teaching and learning experiences in which group participation is used in a variety of ways, and in which discussions approach issues in different ways. Don't let habit keep you from trying some of the variety, or from involving the group in participation in ways that might not be familiar to you. In this course you are primarily a leader, not a teacher. As leader you strive to arrange for the learning to take place, but the members of the group must teach one another through their study, reading, discussion, and interaction together.

Since so many adults carry an image of children listening obediently to a teacher, they are inclined to think of themselves as passive spectators who must never move their lips. If the members of your group suffer from this malady, let them observe the children's activities—and how the youngsters participate in learning in the kindergarten and primary departments. We all learn in part by doing. Then let them decide what meaningful participation means for them on the adult level. They are not sponges soaking in information, but a community of fellow seekers, each enriching the other.

The leader is not the person with wisdom pouring it into a funnel of minds that are extended before him. The message of the Bible is not learned by having it poured in any more than one can learn to play the piano by being told how to do it. Undoubtedly the piano teacher could always play the new piece better than the pupil, but the pupil doesn't learn to play by hearing the teacher do it and then hearing the teacher express disgust over the fact that the pupil can't repeat it after he was just shown how. To play the piano one must practice under the guidance of another. It is practice, the cultivation of innate talents under the guidance of one more experienced, that produces the skilled musician. So it is with Bible study.

Keep the image of the group as a study group, both in your own mind and in the minds of the members, that they may be conscious of their responsibilities in learning and in sharing in the progress of the sessions.

The general assumption behind most of the suggestions offered is that the study group is a small one of approximately eight to eighteen people. The members are visualized as sitting in a circle, or around a table, or in some other way that enables them to look at each other and to talk together. Sitting in rows makes group participation and interchange almost impossible because members of the group cannot address one another. Sitting in rows is designed only for listening to the teacher who lectures from the front and for asking him questions. All exchange is with the teacher, not from member to member.

The suggestions also assume that the leader has been eager for this kind of group learning procedure. Furthermore, it is hoped that in previous periods the group has developed a familiarity and openness that permits the members to talk freely with each other without hesitation or embarrassment. If such has not been achieved the suggestions in this course are designed to help the leader proceed in developing this kind of free participation. Such participation depends most often on the approach and attitude of the leader. Good questions asked by the leader that frankly face issues and that *do not have obvious answers* are important for promoting discussion. Furthermore, it is important that the leader also pose those problem questions for which he doesn't have a clear or the only answer. This enables the group to realize that they participate in the teaching as well as in the learning process. It also engenders mutual growth.

To achieve the kind of class conceived the leader must exhibit a willingness to listen to and accept the comments of others. Then this will eventually happen among the group members as well. The contribution of each must be received and the leader must have the ability to pick out the relevant and the significant ideas, as well as the ability to draw the discussion together with a succinct summary which gathers up the conclusion of the group. If the leader will recapitulate the argument, and then focus the discussion by indicating the problem at which the group has arrived, or the insight it has gained, the session will have order and movement.

THOUGHTS FOR THE LEADER

A quotation appears at the beginning of each session of this coursebook. At various places the session suggestions speak of these as the Thought for the Leader. These quotations are meant for the leader to meditate upon and for him to use occasionally as resource material for sessions of the study group.

UNIT I

the nature and use of the parables

One of the most helpful things that the leader can do is to keep the group aware of the direction of the course by recalling what the previous session or sessions were and where the present session leads. At the end of the session a brief comment on how the following session fits into the overall plan will be helpful.

The discussion under the introduction to each unit is designed to help the leader keep this overall view.

The first unit helps the group find out what a parable is and how to interpret it. Session 1 raises the question of how a parable should be interpreted, by citing an historical interpretation that is radically different from most modern ones, and then by encouraging the group to read a parable to find out what it means.

The second session offers a description of the nature of the parables and the techniques they use to make their points. We consider what to look for in reading them.

Session three turns the focus from the parable itself to the audience. The meaning of the parable relates specifically to the people to whom it is addressed. This session explores how the application of the parable varies with the kind of people addressed.

Session four is an optional session that may be used to deal with unfinished items. In this session we are concerned not with how the audience determines the application as much as with how other materials grouped with the parable by the gospel writer help us to understand the meaning he saw in the parable.

Summary: To interpret a parable we must understand (1) the techniques of parable writing, (2) its original audience, and (3) the materials with which the gospel writer has placed it.

what is a parable?

For the parables have an arresting
quality which has etched them deep in
memory. They are based on things seen, and
they awake immediate and vivid images which
are seen again in the mind. As John
Bunyan knew, the citadel of Man-Soul is
stormed more easily through eye-gate
than through ear-gate; and it is
because they enter through the visual
imagination that the parables have
penetrated so surely into the
thought and conscience of
innumerable folk. Into the
thought and also into the
conscience, be it noted, for the
parables provoke far more than curiosity.
They not only arrest attention;
they arouse something deep within.

—W. R. Bowie in *The Interpreter's Bible*[1]

The citadel of Man-Soul is stormed more easily through eye-gate than through ear-gate.

PURPOSE OF THIS SESSION

In this session we are concerned with the introduction of the course and with the questions: What is a parable? How is it to be read to discover the meaning that Jesus intended? The parable is a literary form that has its own special characteristics, and these must be understood before parables can be interpreted rightly. This session is designed to lead members of the group to recognize this by the raising of difficult questions. It is a session designed to raise rather than to answer questions.

BEGINNING THE SESSION

Why are we in this course?

Our first task is to arrive at some understanding of the purpose of our course, preferably in a written statement of purpose. There are numerous ways in which this might be approached. One would be to begin this first session by asking members of the group to respond to the question, Why are we in this course? This might be a group discussion, or it might consist of asking each person to talk with a group neighbor or two for a few minutes, or the question might be posted and persons asked to write their answers on sheets of paper. If you elect one of the latter two approaches you will want to follow with a brief group discussion. These two ways will give vastly more participation, but will also consume more time.

Another way to introduce the course and to arrive at an understanding of its purpose would be for you or a member or members of the group to have prepared (preferably in writing—on chalkboard, poster or newsprint) a preliminary statement of course purpose. This would give the group the benefit of some preliminary thought, and would serve as a stimulus for response. If you do it this way you might seek group opinion by asking a question or questions such as: Is this the kind of purpose we really want and should have for this course? How can our statement of course purpose be strengthened? What should this course do for us in the achievement of its goals? What should *we* do to insure success for the course?

The next phase of the session would be a brief description of the nature and purpose of the first of the four units of the course. You will want each member of the group to understand that this first unit concerns itself with the nature and use of the parables. You may want to distribute copies of the outline of the units on page 11 of this book. If so you will need to have them duplicated.

By this time it will have become important to turn the activity of the group to an examination of the resource book, *Exploring the Parables*. Ask them to look at the table of contents. After allowing sufficient time for a thoughtful glance over the table of contents, ask members of the group to examine the appendix. Indicate that this is an important aid in the study of the parables.

If the use of such a resource book is unfamiliar to members of the group, you will want to say something about the design of the resource book. See pages 8–9 of this coursebook for background information. The important thing for them to understand is that the resource book is a reading and study book in which it is possible and highly desirable for persons to read ahead of the section discussed in group sessions. It is a regular paperback book that should be read in its entirety as early in the course as it is possible for members of the group to do so.

After introducing the course in these ways, go back to the question about what *members* can do to make this study of the parables most significant. Be sure to draw as many persons as possible into the discussion. Especially to be desired is the attitude that each member can contribute. Also encourage the group to reflect on the parables during the week and to think about the relevance of the parables to everyday events. News of current events, literature, and the arts may well throw light on a parable previously studied or provide a new application of it. Such activity will help your study become alive.

Have a recorder note the ideas of the ways that members of the group can contribute to the study of the parables. Have him write them on a blackboard, or if possible more permanently on newsprint, as you gather them. Then the group can look back at these suggestions from time to time during the course to discover whether you are profiting from all the possible opportunities for learning. It will be well for you to review the possibilities several times during the course and to make sure that all of the more constructive suggestions are utilized.

DEVELOPING THE SESSION

Once a sense of the course and the group's participation in it has been gained, proceed by having the group read Augustine's treatment of the parable of the good Samaritan. It is on pages 7–8 of the resource book, *Exploring the Parables*. Let the group discuss their reaction to this exposition. Is this the meaning that they have been accustomed to find in this parable? Do they feel that Augustine has grasped what Jesus intended by the story? Why does the resource book call Augustine's treatment "a classic example" of allegorizing? If they think that Augustine's treatment is wrong, what did he do that caused him to go astray, and how can this be avoided?

After the group has wrestled with this treatment and perhaps begun to come to some degree of understanding of the difficulties and dangers in interpreting parables, have them read the parable of the seed growing of itself (Mark 4: 26–29) at the beginning of chapter one of the resource book. Let them discuss the meaning that they see in the parable. There might be wide divergence over this, but encourage free and frank discussion. If the group does not, the leader can raise the question of how we can know what Jesus meant to say by the parable.

The introduction of the course, the discussion of Augustine's approach, and the discussion of the parable of the seed growing of itself will more than consume the available time—and leave many unanswered questions. In this first session it is more important to raise questions that interest and involve persons than to answer all their concerns.

SUMMARIZING THE SESSION

In your summary, point out the significant ideas or problems raised in the discussions of (1) Augustine's interpretation of the parable of the good Samaritan, and (2) of the parable of the seed growing of itself. It is not desirable to try to have neat answers. The summary might best point out questions that have been raised which the group will want to keep in mind during the coming sessions. Record the pertinent questions raised so that they can be reviewed later in the course in order to see if they have been adequately answered.

It is always well to have a summary statement that draws things together by indicating what was covered and what remains to be done. It might be a good practice during the entire course if you would occasionally call upon an able person to make the summary statement at the conclusion of the session. Such a practice trains people to see the movement in the group process. If this procedure is a new one to your group, it would be well to ask persons before the sessions begin, so that they will not be flustered by the suddenness of the request.

ASSIGNMENT

You will want to hold up a copy of the resource book *Exploring the Parables* as you recall what you said earlier about reading and studying it in its entirety as early as possible. The next session will be concerned with matters dealt with in chapters one and two of the resource book, so that every member of the group will want to come with a knowledge of these. Ask members of the group to write down these two questions for consideration in their study of chapters one and two:

I. What is the difference between a parable and an allegory? How would you define an allegory?

II. What light do the techniques and features of parables throw upon understanding and interpreting them?

An understanding of the nature and use of parables is greatly enhanced by an examination of listings of the parables of Jesus. The appendixes of the resource book and of this coursebook give such listings. In order for the group to see that lists vary according to one's definition of parables (and because the dividing lines become quite thin) it is highly desirable to compare these resource book listings with others. Ask a member—or preferably two or three—of the group to come to the next session prepared to lead the group in such a comparison. A major portion of the preparation for such leadership will consist of making available to the group the comparative lists on pages 126–128 of this coursebook. These lists could be lettered onto posters or duplicated for distribution at the next session.

THINKING OVER THE CLASS SESSION

After this first session (and subsequent sessions) the leader should review what happened. This will have the value of helping him become aware of teaching opportunities, as well as of ways to make the sessions more meaningful to the members. Let the leader think about the following questions.

1. *Where any ideas expressed or questions asked that should be pursued in subsequent study sessions?* These can be used as opportunities for further learning.

2. *Did all members of the group participate freely or are some reticent?* If so, do they have special interests and skills that can be used in following weeks?

3. *Did the leader dominate the session or talk too much?* Was he open to the ideas of others and willing to listen as well as respond?

4. *Was the setting in the room such that members could participate freely and talk with each other as well as with the leader?* Are there ways in which the setting in the room can be improved?

5. *Was there movement in the discussion?* Was this evident to the members of your group? In what ways could the leader have focused the problem and aided in the progress of the discussion? How will the early portion of the next session recall and summarize today's session?

ADDITIONAL RESOURCES

As indicated on page 16 of this coursebook, we have endeavored to make this a self-contained course, complete and effective without additional reference volumes. We do give additional resources, however, for those persons who desire them. Especially do we list the volumes of *The Interpreter's Bible,* because these are often available to adult study groups from church or pastoral libraries.

1. "The Parables," by W. R. Bowie in *The Interpreter's Bible,* Vol. VII, pp. 165–175, makes good supplementary reading and helpful information for discussion. It would be helpful for this volume to be available as a reference at all sessions of this course.

2. A sermon entitled "The Parable of the Seed Growing Secretly," beginning on page 83 of *The Waiting Father* by Helmut Thielicke, is concerned with the parable discussed in chapter one of the resource book.

3. B. T. D. Smith in *The Parables of the Synoptic Gospels,* pp. 35–41, discusses the characteristics of parables as forms of popular story telling and indicates their extensive use of parallel statement. These pages give extensive background on the literary form of the parables.

THE RICH YOUNG MAN

ROGER MARTIN

session 2

learning to read
a parable

Now, Reader, I have told my dream to thee;
See if thou canst interpret it to me,
Or to thyself, or neighbour; but take heed
Of misinterpreting; for that, instead
Of doing good, will but thyself abuse:
By misinterpreting evil ensues.

Take heed also that thou be not extreme,
In playing with the outside of my dream:
Nor let my figure or similitude
Put thee into a laughter or a feud.
Leave this for boys and fools; but as for thee,
Do thou the substance of my matter see.

Put by the curtains, look within my veil,
Turn up my metaphors, and do not fail,
There, if thou seekest them, such things to find,
As will be helpful to an honest mind.

—Bunyan [1]

PURPOSE OF THIS SESSION

In this session we are exploring how understanding the general characteristics of a parable contributes to the interpretation of the basic idea of the parable. Does the knowledge of the nature of the parable throw any light on some of the questions that were raised last week.

BEGINNING THE SESSION

Call for ideas that came to members of the group during their everyday lives because of the previous session's discussion. Have at least one idea of your own to contribute.

Let the members who studied the listings of parables report on what variations they discovered. Members of the group, or those making the report, can discuss any surprises they had in terms of what are parables.

DEVELOPING THE CLASS SESSION

Have the class read Mark 4: 26–29 again, then discuss the interpretation of the parable that was given in the resource book, pp. 9–11. Let the group express their reaction to the book, and see if they can understand the reason for the interpretation given. Any persons that have done additional reading can contribute their insights to this discussion. Turn to the application of the parable on p. 11 of the resource book and let the group discuss it. Do they see any further applications of the parable? What is the difference between the interpretation of the parable and its application?

Turn to techniques of oral stories and functional features of parables given on pp. 16–21 of the resource book. Try to determine which of these are illustrated by the parable of the seed growing of itself. Discuss each of these techniques and these functional features thoroughly and relate each one to the interpretation of parables. In discussing the techniques of the oral story, try to find out if anyone can give additional examples of the five characteristics. These can be taken from other parables or from traditional oral stories such as "The Three Bears," "The Three Little Pigs," and fairy tales.

Before proceeding with the course make sure that all are beginning to understand what a parable is, and how they can distinguish it from other forms of teaching. Let members of the group distinguish in their own words between the following forms of teaching:

1. a proverb
2. an illustration
3. a metaphorical story (parable)
4. an allegory

Ask that they also give examples of each. They might obtain some of these from pp. 7–16 of the resource book.

The most important and probably the most difficult distinction to make is between an allegory and a parable. A number of New Testament parables have been interpreted as allegories throughout history because of confusion on this distinction. An example is on page 7 of the resource book and can be used here to help clarify the distinction. Read and discuss the allegories given in order to find out how they differ from parables in technique and method of interpretation. What happens when a parable is read as if it were an allegory?

Ask the members of the group to tell their conception of a parable. A wide divergence will indicate the necessity of further clarification before the parables can be clearly interpreted. If there is a growing clarity on this point, the leader will know he can proceed. Closely related to this basic question are the questions as to the purpose of a parable, and how a parable accomplishes its purpose. Some ideas on all of these questions ought to be expressed in the general discussion. If the discussion includes them all you need not press each question, but it would be well to sum up the ideas so that the group may see more clearly what has been said.

It is important for the leader always to summarize the ideas expressed in any discussion, in order that the group may see the gist of their thinking. Otherwise the discussion will appear to have revealed nothing to the participants and will not provide an incentive or a focus for further questioning or understanding. The danger in discussion is the feeling that it gets nowhere. Someone who can pick out the significant ideas and trace the development of thought can help everyone see what has happened through the process of the group.

Have the group read Mark 4: 11–12 in the light of their answers to the question: What is the purpose of the parables? Let them decide whether the ideas expressed in these verses are consistent with their previous concept of the purpose of the parables. Let all face honestly the problems in understanding what a parable is that are raised by this verse, and express any difficulties that they have with the words.

If the group seems to bypass the difficulties of Mark 4: 11–12 too readily (the verses seem to say that the purpose of parables is to conceal the truth from outsiders), it is the duty of the leader to continue raising questions that force the group to face the implications of the statement. Only if this is done will they formulate a deep enough comprehension of the meaning of the parables for them to be able to deal with and answer the questions of others who confront them outside these study sessions. Furthermore, if subsequently their Christian faith is challenged, they will have inner resources of discipline and understanding to meet the challenge.

An alternate possibility in developing this session would be to take the Old Testament passages that are mentioned in chapter two of the resource book and read them during this session in order to discuss what they reveal about the background of the parable form of teaching. Some insight into the nature of the parable can be obtained from a knowledge of the forerunners of Jesus' parables. Let the group discuss why Jesus took an old form of teaching and developed it, rather than attempting something distinctive and new.

SUMMARIZING THE SESSION

Set forth the understanding of the parable that the group has achieved. It will be interesting to observe whether the group's conception of the parable has changed as a result of these first two sessions, and if so, how much. Is there a more precise understanding of what a parable is and how it should be interpreted? If so, in what ways is it more precise?

ASSIGNMENT

Ask that all members of the group reflect on what has been discussed in these sessions on the nature and purpose of parables. It would be helpful if each person would follow up this session by *writing*, in his own words, a description of the nature and purpose of parables.

Remind the group that the next session will assume that they have studied chapter three of the resource book. This chapter is on the influence of "The Life Situation" on the message and interpretation of parables.

THREE SECTIONS OF BACKGROUND INFORMATION

SECTION A

In the sermon by Thielicke on the parable of the seed growing secretly there are some remarks that can be used as a basis for discussion of the application of the parable after its meaning has been interpreted. Man is in control with his modern scientific powers.

"Why does he worry? Because now there is nobody there upon whom he can cast his cares. Why is he active and overwatchful? Because he no longer sees the eyes that watch over him. Why can't he sleep? Because he can no longer let himself go. For the world has become a weird place. Whatever happens without him and when he is not there himself he cannot trust. So he has to be everywhere. . . . We . . . are no longer able to *let* things happen. For this you can do only if you know that somebody is in control and if you know who that somebody is." [2]

SECTION B

Oesterley makes the following comments in comparing the parables of Jesus with the parables currently told at that time by Jewish rabbis.

"The great majority of the Rabbinical parables are exegetical; they purport to explain difficulties in the Scriptures, and especially in the Pentateuch; the exaltation of the Law, and the need of observing its ordinances are very often the purpose of these parables. Unlike the few parables found in the Old Testament, and unlike so many of those in the Gospels, the Rabbinical parables are not prompted by surrounding circumstances; they have not, that is to say, the practical value of these; a great many have merely a theoretical interest, useful for the students of Scripture in the Rabbinical schools, but of little help to the masses." [3]

While the Jewish parables are used to illuminate or explore an authoritative text by the teachers, the parables of Jesus are not explanations of something else, but they are the message and preaching of Jesus himself. Because they are the message itself, they are not illustrative stories to be heard, but they involve the hearer as an actor or participant who must respond to the challenge—"Which one of you . . .?"

SECTION C

Allegorizing is a form of interpretation that was used extensively by the ancient Greeks. It is thought to have been developed so that Greek people of later days could read Homer without being offended by the crudities and amorous affairs of the gods and goddesses on Mount Olympus. Homer had achieved the religious status of being the "bible" of the Greeks. As men became more civilized, they were offended by the tales unless they could read them allegorically and find in them some spiritual meaning.

Philo used this method to reconcile Hebrew religion with Greek philosophy. By reading Genesis allegorically he could, for example, identify the rivers of the garden of Eden with the Stoic virtues, thereby overcoming the differences in the two approaches to life.

Although there are a few examples of Paul's use of allegory (Galatians 4), and other parables in the early Christian period, it came into prominence only when men were converted in large numbers from the Greek world. Although we have a few indications that the parables were occasionally looked at allegorically by the first generation of Christians, the allegorical interpretation of the parables expanded in subsequent centuries. It persisted to the time of the reformation as the chief way of interpreting the parables. Protestant reformers Luther and Calvin saw allegory as disguising the plain meaning of scripture, and therefore rejected the absolute hold of the Greek tradition. The justification given for the allegorical interpretation of scripture was that it enabled the reader to find some deep and hidden spiritual meaning in all of the words of Jesus, down to their last detail.

A. M. Hunter, in chapter two of his *Interpreting the Parables,* gives something of the history of the way the church has used the parables, including a number of examples of the allegorical interpretation. The chief tendency was to find Christ as the object of a number of the symbols. He was thought to be what was symbolized by such references as the mustard seed that is sprouting, the good Samaritan, and the wise builder upon the rock.

Since the church had no historical perspective toward scripture, but interpreted it all as on one level with no distinction between the Old Testament and the New Testament, it became convenient to use allegory to deal with those passages, especially of the Old Testament, that seemed unworthy of God. Thus, allegory became the accepted method of finding the "deeper" meaning of particular passages of scripture.

The great allegorists in the early Christian tradition came from the Hellenistic city of Alexandria, where Greek learning and Philo had established a strong precedence for allegory. Clement of Alexandria and Origen, both active at the beginning of the third century, were the chief introducers of extreme allegory in the Christian tradition. It must be said in their defense that while their method was wrong, they believed the scripture to be God's word, and searched diligently for its deepest meaning.

Yet there was a school of interpreters at Antioch who kept before them the plain sense of the words as the true meaning of one scripture, and who opposed the search for hidden meanings. Chrysostom, the great orator of the ancient church, usually succeeded in going to the heart of the meaning of the parable without getting sidetracked in innumerable details, or in making the parts of the story symbols for unlimited possibilities. Even in the early church, allegory did not go unchallenged.

the life situation of the parable

By striving at every possible point to make itself
intelligible, the talk has sought to bring these
things within the reach of each listener.
But the intelligibility of the talk, and the
listener's understanding of it, are
still not the talk's true aim.
This by no means gives the meditation
its proper emphasis. For in order
to achieve its proper emphasis the talk
must unequivocally demand
something of the listener. . . . now the talk
must unconditionally demand the reader's
own decisive activity, and all depends upon this.

—Kierkegaard[1]

PETER SCHLAIFER

PURPOSE OF THIS SESSION

The parables of Jesus were applied to the situation in which the hearer lived. In this session we endeavor to understand what this means in reading a parable, and how the basic meaning gains new relevance as it is applied to new situations. Although every parable has only one point, the *situation of the hearer* or reader is crucial for its application. Men in different situations will apply the same message differently, depending upon their circumstances. These are the propositions we seek to investigate in this session.

BEGINNING THE SESSION

As a review of the first two chapters, the leader may recall how parables lead the hearer to judge himself. The situation of the hearer is an important ingredient in the total context of meaning. *Two elements are always involved:* (1) *The meaning of the parable—*what did the *speaker* intend to say? (2) *The situation of the hearer—*how does the basic message apply to his *circumstances of life?*

Neither of these elements is sufficient in itself. The meaning of a parable is complete only when it reaches into the life of the reader. This double facet is clearly illustrated in the New Testament parables themselves. The first two chapters of the resource book dealt with ascertaining the meaning of parables as *intended by the speaker*. The third chapter gets at the question of how the *situation of the hearer* is always vital in making the parable relevant to the life situation. The issue that we introduce in this session is how the parables of Jesus are given specific and vivid applications according to the situations of the hearers. The parable does not give a general truth, but wrestles with someone's specific attitude, problem, fault, or characteristic. A parable always scores a direct hit!

DEVELOPING THE SESSION

In this and in coming sessions the basic reading tool is the Bible itself. We are concerned with getting members of the group to feel at ease in reading the Bible and in being able to feel that they can come to its meaning regardless of their preconceived expectations. In the previous two sessions a Bible passage has been a vital part of the discussion, and in the sessions that follow this pattern ought to become more and more significant, because we interpret specific parables.

Have the group examine the two settings of the parable of the lost sheep (Matthew 18: 12–14 and Luke 15: 3–7). As the resource book points out, notice how the group of people to whom the parable is addressed varies in the two gospels. These two groups of people live in two different circumstances of life. It ought not be surprising that the thrust which the parable makes takes on a different dimension as it is applied to each of these groups. The message of the parable is the same, but its implications vary for hearers in altered circumstances.

Consider the two groups of hearers and discuss how each would apply the parable to itself. Let the study group speculate on other possible modern groups of readers of the parables and how each—if conscientious—would apply the parable to itself. For example, what application does the parable have to a congregation of Christians in your particular circumstances? What application to modern America?

The resource book suggests an application to those in our world who are "lost." An application to this group of hearers is not made in the Bible itself. Let the class discuss whether the resource book's application to the "lost" is valid. Does a parable like the lost sheep provide various applications for the same person as his situation is seen from differing perspectives? When the group discussed the parable's application to your congregation or to modern America, was there one single application, or did the discussion reveal several possible applications as the group was seen from differing perspectives?

The filmstrip on the parable of the lost sheep may be used here. Follow the showing with a discussion of the meaning that it gives to the parable. Does the filmstrip adequately communicate the idea that the parable in Luke was told *to rebuke those who oppose Jesus,* rather than to console the distressed? Would we be as inclined to sentimentalize about the love of God if we remembered the context of this and the other parables in Luke 15? Let the class discuss whether the filmstrip presents this original context, or whether it has left this context behind and generalized the parable so that man today would not see it as carrying an implied criticism. If it is decided that the filmstrip misses this original context, does the group approve or do you feel that something has been lost in the process?

This session has been designed to suggest the importance of the setting given to the parables of the New Testament. We must know who *the hearers* are before any parable can be rightly applied and its relevance determined. When Jesus told parables they spoke to the needs of the people he knew. When we use the parables we must not only be aware of their meanings, but also of the needs of the people with whom we deal.

If there is still time, consider another example of a parable that is given application in two different settings in the gospels. Follow a procedure similar to the one outlined above for determining how the *situation of the hearers* gives a different application to the parable of the defendant (Luke 12: 57–59 and Matthew 5: 23–26).

SUMMARIZING THE SESSION

Have one of the group summarize the ideas that seem significant to him as a result of this discussion dealing with the application of the same parable to different groups both in the New Testament and in modern times.

ASSIGNMENTS

Ask two persons to interview five members of the congregation in an attempt to discover what "the kingdom of God" means to the average church member. Tell the two interviewers that you will receive their report as a prominent part of the group's forthcoming study of the parables of the kingdom.

If optional session four is to be used there will be no additional assignment in the resource book other than a reminder to study the book as early in the course as possible. If optional session four is to be omitted assign the first part of chapter four of the resource book, pp. 37–41.

BACKGROUND INFORMATION

Finding the sayings of Jesus in more than one setting in the gospels is an extensive practice, and in this section we propose to give more examples for the leader to study.

The saying, "A good tree bears good fruit," is reported twice in the Gospel of Matthew. In the first instance it is addressed to the disciples and the crowd (in the sermon on the mount, Matthew 7: 16–20), while in the second instance it is addressed to the Pharisees (Matthew 12: 33–37). The first saying gives a test by which the multitude or the disciple can discern the false prophets. The second is a judgment of the Pharisees.

The parabolic proverb, "Can the blind man lead a blind man? Will they not both fall into a pit?" is told in Luke 6: 39 to the multitude or the disciples, where it warns them against following the wrong teachers. In Matthew 15: 14 it is also addressed to the disciples, and is in answer to a question about the Pharisees and has the point: Don't worry about the opposition of the Pharisees; they will dig their own grave. They are blind guides and will fall into the pit with those whom they lead. Let them alone.

In Luke 14: 34 the saying about salt is addressed to the multitudes and is applied as a challenge and threat. If salt has lost its taste it is fit to be thrown away. "He who has ears to hear, let him hear" (Luke 14: 35). In Mark 9: 50 it is addressed to disciples, and is a call to inner power and peace: "Have salt in yourselves, and be at peace with one another." Matthew 5: 13 identifies the salt and the disciples: "You are the salt of the earth." The disciples are to flavor the earth. Yet, the threat remains that if salt loses its ability to season society it is good only to be cast out.

ADDITIONAL RESOURCES

If any members of your group desire to do study beyond that of the resource book, you might suggest the following:

1. Hunter, *Interpreting the Parables.*
2. Thielicke, *The Waiting Father.*
3. *The Interpreter's Bible,* Vols. VII and VIII.

session 4*

the context
in the gospel

> For pausing is not a sluggish repose.
> Pausing is also movement. It is the inward
> movement of the heart. To pause is to deepen
> oneself in inwardness. But merely going fur-
> ther is to go straight in the direction of
> superficiality. —Kierkegaard [1]

THINKING OVER THE PREVIOUS SESSIONS

Before planning this session it would be well to take stock of how the group has been making out. Turn back to the questions given under the heading "Thinking Over the Session" at the end of session one.

Have the members become free in their participation in discussions? To get an accurate check you might ask a friend to keep track of how many times each member participates in the discussion during the coming session. A very important related question is: Does any person dominate the discussion and keep others from participating as they might? If so, in what ways can his domination be curbed diplomatically and at the same time give more opportunity to others? Perhaps participation can be more evenly distributed by delegating responsibilities as evenly as possible.

Finally, have the suggestions given in the first session on how members of the group could participate been followed through? Has the group's pace been such that mem-

* An Optional Session

bers can contribute insights that came to them during the week? As the course goes on, opportunities for recollection will enable members to bring in subsequent insights that occurred to them following discussions. All of us have left a study session and felt that we got our most significant insight after the period was over.

PURPOSE OF THIS SESSION

In this session we will explore how the gospel context often gives insights into the meaning of the parables of Jesus. The meaning that a specific parable or saying of Jesus has for a gospel writer is indicated by the other sayings and actions with which it has been grouped and reported.

This session should also provide a good opportunity to catch up on any material that has been omitted from the three introductory sessions and that the group is still unclear about or is interested in. You may even want to spend the whole period clarifying and assimilating the ideas of the first three chapters of the resource book and the unanswered questions that have come up during the first three sessions.

BEGINNING THE SESSION

Call upon the members of the group to contribute any additional insights they may have gained since the last time, or to raise any questions they have about their reading in the resource book.

DEVELOPING THE SESSION

Examine Luke 13: 6–9 to discover how the context of the gospel helps in the interpretation of the meaning of a parable. This matter is discussed under the heading "Thought Context in the Gospel" at the end of chapter three in the resource book.

Throughout the course occasional reference will be made to the context for interpretation. Some of these places are listed below and they can be referred to and studied at this point.

In chapter seven of the resource book, the context of

PETER SCHLAIFER

the parable of the sower is used to gain insight into the meaning of this parable. What emphases does Mark 4: 21–25 give that help suggest something of the context in which the parable of the sower is to be interpreted? Does the fact that this parable is told during the portion of the gospel of Mark in which the kingdom is proclaimed to the multitudes, and is followed by the parables of the kingdom, throw any light upon its meaning? Does the fact that Jesus tells it during the period of his great popularity have any effect on the meaning that we see in it or that comes from it?

Many of the parables are reported in pairs in the gospels. What value might this have for their interpretation? Such pairs are: (1) The rash king and the uncompleted tower, (2) The leaven and the mustard seed; (3) The lost sheep and the lost coin (also the prodigal son); (4) The hidden treasure and the costly pearl. These pairs suggest that the early church and the gospel writers felt that these parables have similar meanings. The point of one helps clarify the point of the other and their differences are largely irrelevant.

If there is time remaining, discuss how the sayings of Jesus addressed to the crowds or his opponents were later applied to the disciples and used for Christian education. A discussion of this fact, especially as it is relevant to the materials that deal with sayings of the coming kingdom and the end, is vital. Reapplication is important but it always introduces the grave danger of altering the message in its new application. Let the group note how sayings of Jesus concerning the imminent coming of the kingdom were reapplied to the second coming and were later used to explain the delay of the second coming. See pp. 33–34 of the resource book.

CONCLUDING THE SESSION

Toward the end of the session ask each person to take five to ten minutes to write a statement in the session on his understanding of the kingdom of God. The leader can provide paper and pencils. Assure the group that the statements will not be read until they are returned after the study sessions of the kingdom of God. At that time each person will be called upon to evaluate his original statement and describe any ways in which his ideas have grown as a result of careful study of the biblical parables themselves. This activity will help to give insight into the learning that is taking place during the course and will be helpful to the leader in assessing the group's development. It will also provide the group members with interesting insights into their own concepts. Writing down the ideas is very important. Otherwise we tend to feel that we would have said just what we now discern. The written statement enables each person to look at his former opinion and evaluate it objectively.

ASSIGNMENT

Tell the group that we are to consider the parable of the laborers in the vineyard (Matthew 20: 1–16).

Two or three group members might each be asked to prepare to lead in a consideration of the background and the terms of the parable of the laborers in the vineyard.

Inform them that they will be called upon to explain such unusual terms as "the third hour," "denarius," and the prominence of the marketplace, as well as to throw light on the Palestinian labor practices that are reflected in the parable.

The group assignment is chapter four of the resource book, pages 37–41, unless session six is to be omitted, in which case the whole of chapter four should be assigned.

ADDITIONAL RESOURCES

You might be prepared to offer suggestions as to the source of information about the parable of the laborers in the vineyard. Included might be the resource book, a Bible dictionary, and a commentary such as volume seven of *The Interpreter's Bible.*

There is a sermon on the parable of the laborers in the vineyard in *The Waiting Father,* by Helmut Thielicke.

UNIT II

parables of the kingdom

We are now ready to deal with the message of the parables. In this course the parables are grouped according to their various subjects. Because the kingdom of God is the primary subject of both the parables of Jesus and of his teaching and healing, we begin by discussing the parables of the kingdom.

Sessions one and two deal with the grace of God. In session one this is communicated under the theme of the kingdom of God as a gift. In session two the subject used to convey the same idea is an invitation to the wedding feast. The starting point in the parables of the kingdom is what God does—his grace.

Sessions three and four deal with the way in which the kingdom operates in the present time. Session three suggests that the kingdom is hidden and hard to discern and yet has such power that the future belongs to it. Session four is set in the context of the grace of God, that is as freely given as a gift or an invitation. This session stresses that for the time being the kingdom of God encompasses all kinds of people. The decision of who is worthy among those gathered is left to God, at a time of his choosing.

Although sessions three and four deal primarily with the working of the kingdom in the present, they also proclaim that God controls the future. Sessions five and six discuss the parables that deal primarily with God's control of the future, although they also have implications for the present. The future fulfillment of God's purpose entails present-day repentance and heightened responsibility for those who sense the crisis. The concluding session (six) of Unit II considers the judgment of God—who assumes complete authority in the end—and what this means for our lives, both at the present time and in the future.

PETER SCHLAIFER

'Tis only God may be had for the asking.

session 1

the gift of the

kingdom

At the devil's booth are all things sold,
Each ounce of dross costs its ounce of gold;
   For a cap and bells our lives we pay,
Bubbles we buy with a whole soul's tasking:
   'Tis heaven alone that is given away,
'Tis only God may be had for the asking.

—James Russell Lowell[1]

PURPOSE OF THIS SESSION

This session, based on the parable of the laborers in the vineyard (Matthew 20: 1–16), discusses the meaning of the kingdom of God and seeks to discover how this phrase describes the activity of God. Because the parables are the most distinctive of the preserved forms of Jesus' teaching, they take us close to Jesus' original message. Because of their number they also give us a good representation of Jesus' teaching. With such a basic means for discerning the essence of the gospel, it is significant to find that so many of the parables deal with the kingdom of God. As a result you will want to come to an awareness of the centrality of the kingdom in Jesus' teaching.

BEGINNING THE SESSION

If session four of Unit I was not used, begin by asking the group to write their concept of the kingdom of God as it is discussed near the end of the section entitled, "Developing the Session" in session four of Unit I. Indicate that these will be returned later in the course in order that each person may evaluate his own, and estimate in what ways the study of the parables has enlarged his understanding of the kingdom.

Receive the report of those who interviewed members of the congregation to discern what seems to be the image of the kingdom of God among the members of the church. This is to be used for setting the stage for the discussion, as well as for raising the question as to whether the Christian today has a true picture of the kingdom.

DEVELOPING THE SESSION

Begin with a discussion of the phrase "kingdom of God." Use the opening paragraphs in chapter four of the resource book as the basis for this discussion. How can we achieve the sense of the kingdom as an activity of God instead of a state of being? How does this compare with the conception held by the members of the congregation?

There are listed below a number of possible suggestions for conducting the session. They are not listed in any order, neither can they all be used.

1. Read Matthew 20: 1–16 and discuss its meaning. What are the issues involved in discerning the central point of the parable of the laborers in the vineyard?

2. To whom did Jesus speak the parable and what application did it have? Matthew has it placed so that it would seem to be related to Peter's question in Matthew 19: 27. What meaning would it have in that context? This is a case where a parable seems to have been recorded in the scripture without giving the details of to whom Jesus addressed it and, therefore, what its actual application is to be. Yet some evidence can emerge from the parable itself.

3. Have the group imagine that they are Pharisees hearing the parable for the first time. How does it strike them? For maximum results ask someone to look up material on the Pharisees and their beliefs.

4. In the saying, "Fear not, little flock, for it is your Father's good pleasure to give you the kingdom" (Luke 12: 32) how is the gift of the kingdom related to the injunction "fear not"? Could the parable of the laborers in the vineyard have—in any way—the application of "fear not"?

5. What application does the parable have to business and economic life? Is it more applicable to this sphere than to other spheres of human life?

6. Oesterley, *The Gospel Parables in the Light of Their Jewish Background,* quotes the following Jewish parable.

> ". . . It is like a king who hired many labourers. And there was one labourer who understood his work beyond measure well. What did the king do? He caused him to accompany him as he strolled along many pathways. When evening was come those labourers drew near to receive their wage; and he gave each the full amount of his wage. But the labourers murmured and said, 'We have toiled the whole day, and this man has toiled but two hours, and yet he has given him the same wage as we have received.' Then spake the king to them, 'He has done more work in two hours than ye have during the whole day.' "[2]

Let someone tell this Jewish parable, read it, or make it available in some other way. Ask the group to compare its point of view to that of Jesus' parable. The *form* of the two parables is similar but the *point* is quite opposite. In the Jewish parable everything depends upon what a man deserves as the result of his own effort. How does this compare with the way of God? *What is the one point of Jesus' parable of the laborers in the vineyard?*

The parable of the laborers in the vineyard was extensively allegorized in early Christian history, and some of this temptation occasionally recurs. The form of the allegory took two directions. At times the various hours of the day were symbols of periods of biblical history from Adam to Christ, the people of which came to salvation at different times; at other times they represented the different stages in life at which a man might repent and come to the gospel. A. M. Hunter, *Interpreting the Parables,* reports the venerable Bede's (673–735) treatment of this parable:

> "The householder is God; the vineyard is the Church; the hired men, the saints of all ages; and the penny, the divinity of Christ." [3]

It might be stimulating for the leader to suggest these ideas in seriousness during the session in order to see how persons react to them.

ASSIGNMENTS

Ask that everyone look for material or issues to which the parable of the laborers in the vineyard has relevance.

Session two of Unit II is based on the parables of the invitation to the banquet (marriage feast) in Matthew 22: 1–11 and Luke 14: 15–24 and the wedding garment in Matthew 22: 11–14. If this session is to be used, ask that everyone study these parables in the Bible, with pp. 41–45 of the resource book as commentary. If the session is to be omitted, make the assignment suggested at the end of session two, Unit II.

ADDITIONAL RESOURCES

There is helpful resource material on the parables of the invitation to the banquet (marriage feast) and the wedding garment in volumes seven and eight of *The Interpreter's Bible.*

session 2*

the kingdom as an invitation

Almighty Father, who dost give
   The gift of life to all who live,
Look down on all earth's sin and strife,
   And lift us to a holier life.
—John Howard Masterman[1]

PURPOSE OF THIS SESSION

The kingdom of God is pictured not only as a gift but also as an invitation. In this session we will study the meaning of the figure of an invitation. Furthermore, what effect does this stress on the free gift or invitation seem to have on the concept of human responsibility?

The session is based on the parables of the invitation to the banquet (marriage feast) in Matthew 22: 1–11 and Luke 14: 15–24 and the wedding garment in Matthew 22: 11–14.

BEGINNING THE SESSION

Have the members of the group suggest ideas, experiences, or items that they have noted since the time of the previous session that contributed to their understanding of the relevance of the parable of the laborers of the vineyard.

DEVELOPING THE SESSION

Draw upon the following suggestions for conducting this session's discussion:

1. How is the parable of the invitation to the banquet (marriage feast) in Matthew 22: 1–11 and Luke 14: 15–24 similar to, and how does it vary from, the laborers in the vineyard?

* An Optional Session

PETER SCHLAIFER

2. Compare the two settings of the invitation to the banquet (marriage feast). Let the members of your group imagine that they are the man at table with Jesus and that they made the pious remark (Luke 14: 15). Would they grasp the force of the parable immediately? Would they be offended at such a sharp answer to what was both religious and well-meaning? Is it fair to criticize pious talk? Is such talk a problem for sincere religion today? Notice that the kingdom demands responsibility and that this demand reveals the shallowness of what is mere talk.

3. What if the kingdom of God is a gift? Does this mean that a man can sit back and wait for it, even on his deathbed? Won't he lose his sense of responsibility? If God's gifts come so easily, won't a man lose his incentive for doing good? Doesn't God need to use threats and a get-tough policy? Let the group comment on questions such as these. After some discussion use the prayer that is given under the thought for the leader and see if it reflects any of your thinking or throws any new light on the discussion. Does the prayer express irresponsibility or does it lead to it?

4. Discuss Matthew 22: 11–14. With what additional problems of the church does this short fragment deal? When did problems such as this first arise? What does it suggest about the makeup of the church in Matthew's day? What application do you think it has today?

ASSIGNMENT

The next session is based on the parables of the leaven (Matthew 13: 33 and Luke 13: 20–21) and the mustard seed (Matthew 13: 31–32; Mark 4: 30–32 and Luke 13: 18–19). Ask for the study of these parables with the aid of pages 47–51 of the resource book *Exploring the Parables*.

ADDITIONAL RESOURCES

You might ask someone to read Thielicke's sermon on the parable of the leaven hid in the measure of meal. Be prepared to suggest the page number in the book *The Waiting Father* on which this sermon begins. It is page 61. If you ask someone to read this sermon, ask that he come to the next session prepared to contribute some ideas about the way in which Thielicke applies this parable.

the kingdom:
present and coming

That cause can never be lost or stay'd
Which takes the course of what God hath made,
And is not trusting in walls and towers,
But slowly growing from seed to flowers.[1]

PETER SCHLAIFER

Not trusting in walls and towers,
but slowly growing from seed to flowers.

PURPOSE OF THIS SESSION

The kingdom is described not only as a gift, but is pictured as working in the present and yet waiting to be fulfilled. The next several sessions will be concerned with the kingdom as it relates to this span of time. Some individual parables set forth its present meaning and others describe its coming and future realization. Very often the same parable assumes both of these dimensions. In this session, however, we are concerned with parables that emphasize the operation of the kingdom in the present time. Yet these parables by virtue of contrast also imply a fulfillment that will inevitably come.

The parables on which this session is based are the leaven (Matthew 13: 33 and Luke 13: 20–21) and the mustard seed (Matthew 13: 31–32, Mark 4: 30–32 and Luke 13: 18–19).

BEGINNING THE SESSION

A brief review or summary of the previous two sessions would give perspective to the transition here. This can be done by the leader, by asking members of the group to point out thoughts that have come to them concerning the parable studied in the previous session, or by asking them to recall the most significant ideas of the previous sessions.

After such a discussion you can outline the scope of the coming sessions by indicating the need to relate the kingdom to the present and the future. There are numerous sayings that deal with the kingdom as coming, yet others portray its signs and works in the present time. It can be pointed out that Jesus could say "the kingdom is in your midst," or "at hand," while he taught his disciples to pray, "thy kingdom come."

DEVELOPING THE SESSION

1. Read together and discuss the meaning of the parable of the leaven (Matthew 13: 33; Luke 13: 20–21). Make sure that everyone is clear on what the text is saying before any attempt is made at application to life. In this way the application is more likely to be a true understanding of the gospel of Jesus Christ.

2. Guide the discussion to the relevance of the parable of the leaven to present-day life.

If someone has read the sermon on the leaven hid in the measure of meal in Thielicke's book *The Waiting Father* as suggested in "Additional Resources" at the conclusion of the previous session, ask for a report. This report can become a springboard for others to contribute some ideas of relevance that they find in this parable.

If you did not ask anyone to read and report on this parable (or even if you did), a logical way to proceed would be to divide your group into small groups of five or six persons each. Let these small groups discuss the application of the parable of the leaven. If not discussed before, the relevance that this parable had for its original hearers would also be a suitable topic of discussion for the groups or for the group as a whole. Who were the original hearers? What did the parable mean to them? Don't let the discussions in the small groups run too long, lest they run out of steam. Six to ten minutes should be the time limit. Each group can report on its ideas.

3. If time permits, a discussion of the parable of the mustard seed would be helpful. Try to keep the group from succumbing to the generalization of the mustard as a symbol of faith. The mustard seed and the tree are contrasted in Jesus' parable as an insight into the nature of the kingdom. They are not metaphors for faith.

SUMMARIZING THE SESSION

Have one person summarize what these two parables suggest about the nature of the kingdom of God. Have him indicate the aspect of application that is most relevant to his everyday life.

ASSIGNMENT

Ask three people to go over the parable of the wheat and the tares and gather material for understanding it, using any available resources that deal with its background and its meaning. Ask them to be prepared to begin the next session with a panel discussion on the meaning of the parable, the problems that its interpretation raises, and the relevance that the parable had for its initial audience. If one of the panel members will act the part of the curious person who asks the embarrassing and difficult questions, interest will be heightened. Let the panel discuss frankly the problem raised for interpreters by the allegorical explanation of the parable, and whether this seems to convey the central meaning or not. One of the panel members might interview several people in the church on the meaning of the parable, and represent the general point of view. The other panel member might try to respond with some problems of scholarship raised by the allegorical explanation of this parable.

The next session is based on the parables of the wheat and the tares (Matthew 13: 24–30) and the dragnet (Matthew 13: 47–50). It also calls for a comparison of these parables with the patriarchial story in Genesis 18: 22–33. Ask for a study of these passages with the use of the remainder of chapter five of the resource book, pages 51–55.

BACKGROUND INFORMATION

In chapter five of the resource book we begin to see very clearly how parables that deal with similar subjects are often gathered in groups of two. The existence of pairs probably served as a memory device in the early church, as well as indicating that the early Christians saw a similar meaning in widely different similitudes and stories. A grouping in pairs not only aided the memory, but it also helped to preserve and drive home the central meaning of the parables. Each parable in the pair provides a context of interpretation for the other and prevents an interpretation that goes astray on a detail of the narrative.

ADDITIONAL RESOURCES

1. Some comments on tares in Palestine (Oesterley, *The Gospel Parables in the Light of Their Jewish Background*, pp. 60–62) might be used as background and preparation for next week's session (Compare *The Interpreter's Bible* on Matthew 13: 24–30).

2. Pages 75–79 of Oesterley's book contain background on the mustard seed and plant in Palestine.

session 4

the inclusiveness
of the kingdom

> The talk, which is without author-
> ity, will not have the presumption to
> pass judgment upon you. By vigor-
> ously pondering the occasion you will
> stand before a higher judge, where no
> man dares judge another since he him-
> self is one of the accused.
>
> —Kierkegaard [1]

REVIEW THE PREVIOUS SESSIONS

Review the progress of the course using the questions
for this purpose given in Unit I, pp. 28 and 44.

PURPOSE OF THIS SESSION

The parables of the wheat and the tares (Matthew
13: 24–30) and the dragnet (Matthew 13: 47–50) are difficult because of emphases put on them in the gospel. In
this session we want to interpret them as they throw light
on the working of the kingdom in the present. This session
raises again the relation between an allegory and a parable, and challenges the interpreter to clarify it.

BEGINNING THE SESSION

Have the panel discussion introduce the parable of
the wheat and the tares. As indicated in the previous assignments, let the panel discuss the problems of interpretation raised by the allegorical explanation of this parable.

Following the discussion of the parable by the panel, have the members of the group either ask additional questions of the panel members, or give their own insights into the interpretation. If the opinions of the group differ widely it would be helpful to discuss the reasons for this.

Proceed to a discussion of the relevance of the parable of the wheat and the tares to modern readers. Discuss specifically the four kinds of application suggested in the resource book, pp. 54–55. Point four says that it is often impossible for man to be able to judge his own action for sure. Ask whether anyone can give some situations where a man could not be sure of good or bad when faced with a situation. If this is true, how does a Christian face this fact? How can he go on living in good conscience? If your group is composed of young people or young adults this would be a good opportunity to let them present the problem and then role-play it—having the group members play the roles of the people facing the problem as sincerely and deeply as they can.

If there is time remaining, a discussion of the parable of the dragnet would also be very helpful. This parable raises the difficulty of interpretation that is connected with a number of parables. Have the group observe the similarity between Matthew 13: 40–41 and Matthew 13: 49–50. The form of punishment in Matthew 13: 50 fits the destruction of weeds, but hardly seems appropriate for sorting and throwing away fish. This suggests that the concluding remarks were not originally connected with the parable of the dragnet. In what ways is the parable of the dragnet similar in meaning to the parable of the wheat and the tares?

Read Genesis 18: 22–33 to see if there is a similarity in this patriarchal story to Jesus' parables of the wheat and the tares and the dragnet.

SUMMARIZING THE SESSION

The leader—or someone with whom he has made arrangements in advance—should summarize the basic ideas of the discussion. Since the parables of the wheat and the tares and the dragnet are discussed in the resource book chapter on the "The Kingdom Here and Now" (chapter five), what do these parables contribute to our understanding of the kingdom in the present and in the future? How do the ideas of this pair of parables complement or supplement those of the previous pair of the leaven and the mustard seed?

The summary might also include an observation on what research into the background and knowledge of the parables (such as the wheat and the tares) does for giving a different perspective on meaning. What observations can can be made about the effect of a systematic study of a parable?

ASSIGNMENT

Have everyone prepare for the next session by studying the parable of the ten maidens in Matthew 25: 1–13 and by reading the section in the resource book, pp. 57–59.

Let a panel of three persons be prepared to discuss the application of the parable for our time. This can deal with such questions as the following.

Does the parable encourage us to prepare for the end of the world?

What does it mean to be prepared for any eventuality?

What is the basic distinction between the two types of maidens contrasted in the parable?

ADDITIONAL RESOURCES

Ask someone to read the explanation of the parable of the ten maidens in *The Interpreter's Bible* to explain some of the customs reflected in the parable and to throw light on its development, so that its true-to-life character might be evident for us to whom these ways seem strange. Oesterley, *The Gospel Parables in the Light of Their Jewish Background,* has a much more complete description of the whole wedding procedure that throws light on this parable. See pp. 133–142, especially 133–135.

PETER SCHLAIFER

*. . . till we take the longest
stride of soul man ever took.*

session 5

the crisis

of the kingdom

Thank God our time is now when wrong
Comes up to face us everywhere,
Never to leave us till we take
The longest stride of soul men ever took.
Affairs are now soul size.
The enterprise
Is exploration into God,
Where no nation's foot has ever trodden yet.
. . . It takes
So many thousand years to wake,
But will you wake for pity's sake,
Pete's sake, Dave or one of you,
Wake up, will you?

—Christopher Fry [1]

PURPOSE OF THIS SESSION

The coming of the kingdom is often presented as an impending crisis. The next two sessions strive to bring us to understand the implication that this imminent happening has for the life of the Christian of today who lives centuries after the New Testament was written and expects a long continuation of the world. Does the emphasis on crisis make this aspect of the gospel irrelevant for those of us who expect a continuation of history on earth? Or can the modern believer find a significant dimension added to his earthly existence by the crisis of the kingdom?

Our biblical basis for this session is the parable of the ten maidens (Matthew 25: 1–13).

BEGINNING THE SESSION

If you have had someone do research on the customs of wedding practices that lie behind the parable of the ten maidens (Matthew 25: 1–13), have him explain them and comment on what was learned that throws light on the idea of the procession, barring the door, and other customs.

Since all have read the resource book, the group can raise any questions they have concerning the customs, the meaning of the parable of the ten maidens, or the discussion of it in the resource book.

DEVELOPING THE SESSION

When the group has come to some understanding of the basic issues in the parable, let the panel discuss the significance of the parable for our time. Some of the questions for discussion are given under last week's assignment. Let the members of the panel question each other on points of concern to them. After the panel has had ten minutes of discussion let other members of the group break in and join the questioning or contribute ideas.

Use the statement on page 61 of the resource book concerning Luke 12: 45, that when the Master is not seen as coming, man loses his concern for the present and aligns himself with the forces of evil. When the future does not belong to God the present loses its significance. What is the relation between what is to come and a man's sense of responsibility in the present? Help the group to see how (from the Bible material for this session, Matthew 25: 1–13) the coming of the kingdom as an imminent reality gives a heightened sense of meaning to life as long as the kingdom is also understood as being at work in the world and being concerned for the whole world.

ASSIGNMENTS

The next session will be a study of the story of the last judgment (Matthew 25: 31–46). Ask for a study of the story with the use of pages 63–65 of the resource book.

BACKGROUND INFORMATION

The footnote to Matthew 25: 1 in the Revised Standard Version gives the alternate reading as "Went to meet the bridegroom and the bride." The ancient marriage procession included the bride as well as the groom and probably "and the bride" was dropped by copyists as not belonging to the text during the period when the church interpreted the parable allegorically. This is probably why "and the bride" at the end of Matthew 25: 1 is found in some but omitted from most manuscripts. Later generations which allegorized the parable made Christ the bridegroom. The wise and foolish were viewed as being prepared for the second coming, but they found no place in this for the coming of the bride, who no longer fitted and was consequently forgotten. Thus after the death of Jesus many Christians, probably including the author Matthew himself, allegorized the bridegroom as the figure of Christ and interpreted it as referring to the second coming of Jesus. No longer does the parable stress the judgment and crisis on our life brought by the breaking in of the kingdom, but it becomes a call to patiently watch for the delayed second coming of Christ.

Here we see what happens when allegorical interpretations are read into the text and the parable is made to fit preconceived patterns. The parable as Jesus told it was a lifelike story about a wedding procession and had nothing to do with the second coming, but dealt rather with the crisis that comes with God's breaking into history and with the need for men to be prepared to receive the rule of God in their lives. "Watch therefore" in Matthew 25: 13 is a later comment on the parable that obscures the fact that both the wise and the foolish sleep. It is not the second coming but the crisis of the kingdom that is the subject of this parable.

The parable might well have ended at Matthew 25: 10. Matthew 25: 11–12 are verses that are given elsewhere in other contexts (Matthew 7: 21–23, Luke 13: 25), and these words of Jesus may have been placed with the parable because they fit and reinforce the general idea, "The door was shut." They also carry a hint that Jesus is the gate-keeper or judge.

The parable of the servant placed in authority (Matthew 24: 45–51 and Luke 12: 42–48) also seems to have presented the demand of the kingdom that was about to break in. Peter's question, "Lord, are you telling this parable for us or for all?" (Luke 12: 41) implies that the leaders of the church were one group to whom this parable could be applied, and that the church applied it to its leadership, interpreting it as a caution to the ministry. The false leader is one who takes things into his own hands and self-will on the assumption that the Master is delayed and will therefore not be aware of his specious deeds. Hunter finds the original application to have been to the leaders of Israel, the scribes.

ADDITIONAL RESOURCES

Ask someone to look up background material on the story of the last judgment (Matthew 25: 31–46). There are several Jewish parables that are of a similar nature that can be used. If available, Oesterley, *The Gospel Parables in the Light of Their Jewish Background*, pp. 150–156, presents these Jewish descriptions of the final judgment, as well as raising some interesting insights into the story.

Have another person read the exegesis and the exposition of this parable in *The Interpreter's Bible*, Vol. VII, and be prepared to report on the application of the parable, especially as it is discussed in the exposition. Ask him to comment on whether he feels the application is legitimate and to the heart of the message of the parable.

session 6

the judgment
of the king

While the fact that the kingdom of God is a gift
makes clear that it is the good news of salvation,
the kingdom of God also comes with
a cry of warning and as an announcement
of judgment. The parables of crisis
reveal a people who cannot discern
the signs of the times
and who are rushing to destruction.
As ambiguous as things may be,
we must discern the indicators and glimpse
the signals of God's action in the present,
lest we be destroyed.
The kingdom is not manifestly here;
but its outposts and scouts are already at work,
and these must be recognized.[1]

PURPOSE OF THIS SESSION

What meaning does the story of the last judgment
(Matthew 25: 31–46) have as it relates to our lives and our
world? It might also be observed that this does not have
the usual features of a parable, but presents a descriptive
picture of that which is ultimately important to God. It is a
vision of the end.

PETER SCHLAIFER

*. . . discern the indicators and glimpse
the signals of God's action in the present.*

BEGINNING THE SESSION

Raise the question that was raised last session on how the presence and the coming of the kingdom are related. A discussion of the same question in relation to this parable will permit members of the group to review and to share any insights that they have gained during the week. Pages 65–66 in the resource book present a general summary of the relation of what *is* and what *is to be* in relation to the kingdom. Does the group understand this presentation? What ideas do they get from it?

DEVELOPING THE SESSION

1. This narrative is much like a number of Jewish stories and it would be interesting for the members of the group to report on tales of Judaism that are similar to this one. The group can then point out the similarities and dissimilarities. A good question for the group to discuss is: Why are there Jewish analogies to this story in a way that there are not to the other parables?

2. Let the group proceed to the question: What is the place and meaning of the final judgment in Christianity? Is this parable told to get man to believe in the final judgment? What significance does it have? If you have had someone read the exposition in *The Interpreter's Bible*, ask him to share the insights he discovered there.

3. The parables of the dragnet and the wheat and the tares presented the kingdom gathering all kinds in the present but also implied a final reckoning. Here we have a parable that presents the final reckoning. Does this parable relate to the present and God's rule over it? If the parables of the present do not forget the goal of things, does the parable presenting the goal give a deeper insight into the meaning of the present? Discuss this question.

4. The poem "If Jesus Came Back Today" by Vincent G. Burns, that is given on p. 717 of *Christ and the Fine Arts* can be read and its meaning discussed. It is concerned with whether we are ready to follow Christ in our life.

5. Since this story and the discussion under point four of this section both suggest action, let the group begin to con-

cern itself with what its members might do in a special way to heed the demands that the crisis of the kingdom and the king coming in judgment have upon our lives. Since this question is one that demands some thought, do not press for too hasty a decision. Let them brainstorm for a few minutes about the possibilities. Ask them to think things over so that some clear thinking may arise before the next session.

6. Discuss the following statements from the resource book: "If the kingdom is proclaimed only as a present reality we lose all perspective of God as Judge of the present." "And yet if we only stress the kingdom coming in its fullness, we lose the relevance of the reign of God to life here and now." (Page 65, paragraphs two and four.)

SUMMARIZING THE SESSION

Ask three persons to list what was for them the most significant idea or discovery in this session. You can make the concluding summary by using ideas from the section of the resource book entitled, "The Interdependence of the Present and the Future."

ASSIGNMENT

Have everyone read pp. 63–75 in the resource book. Ask them to think about the meaning of the parable of the last judgment for their lives, as well as to consider what would be appropriate action to express the demand of the coming kingdom.

ADDITIONAL RESOURCES

The final section of *Christ and the Fine Arts* by Cynthia Pearl Maus is entitled "The Inasmuch of Serving." In this section there are pictures and picture interpretations, poetry, stories, and hymns with interpretive comments, which are all on the theme of Christian service. This section provides a variety of resources for conducting the session. Included here is a hymn interpretation of "Where Cross the Crowded Ways of Life" that can provide significant material for discussion related to the theme.

UNIT III

disciples of the kingdom

The kingdom of God gives meaning to man's life at the same time that it lays responsibility upon him. The kingdom as a gift demands use. As present, it means man must live by it. As coming, it suggests that God is Lord of the future and man's life now must be in gear with his ultimate purpose. Unit III deals with the meaning of God's rule in the life of man. It is divided into two parts:

A. The Demands of Discipleship
Session one, "The Ability to Carry Through," suggests that once a disciple embarks on his faith he cannot cease without great trepidation. "No one who puts his hand to the plow and looks back is fit for the kingdom of God" (Luke 9: 62).

Session two, "The Price of Gaining the Kingdom," suggests that the kingdom demands all that one has.

Session three suggests that no man can enter the kingdom of God unless he is willing to run the risk of adventuring into the unknown.

Session four indicates that the disciple lives not by fear of the dangers of failure when he risks all or ventures forth, but by confidence that God's word bears fruit. His confidence is not in himself but that God's word bears fruit.

B. The New Life of Discipleship
The life of a disciple of Jesus Christ is characterized by a transforming relationship. The transforming relationship is between the disciple and God (session five), but out of that new relationship comes a new understanding of one's relations with the material world (session six), with one's neighbor (session seven), and a new understanding of oneself (session eight).

PETER SCHLAIFER

*The demands of discipleship in a world in which
most take religion as something free.*

session 1

the ability
to carry through

These man shares with ox or foal:
The gnaw of hunger, thirst,
And lash of rain are common lot
To flesh and blood accursed
With pain. But this is man's alone:
The search, the deep unrest
Of soul that needs must seek for God—
Inexorable quest!

—Leslie Savage Clark[1]

PURPOSE OF THIS SESSION

In this unit of the course we move from the emphasis on the kingdom as God's gift (which is already inaugurated in the world yet comes in the future and in its coming brings a climactic demand for decision and response) to the other facet of the twofold emphasis. We have been discussing the kingdom as God's. Let us now look at the responsibilities of the man who would live under this rule of God and would respond to the gift of the kingdom. We are now concerned with how man enters the kingdom.

The parables that are the center of interpretation in this session are the dishonest steward (Luke 16: 1–8); the costly tower (Luke 14: 28–30), and the rash king (Luke 14: 31–32). They deal with the cost of entering the kingdom. They present the demands of discipleship in a world in which most take religion as something free—fairly easy, optional for those who like it, as long as they like it—or as synonymous with free will. Freedom of religion has therefore become interchangeable in many persons' minds with the idea that religion is free and easy.

DEVELOPING THE SESSION

In this session you can choose to use either the parable of the dishonest steward or the pair of parables (the costly tower and the rash king) as the main subject. If time allows it is possible to proceed to the other parable as well, but you should make clear the relatedness of these two pieces of scripture.

1. Read the parable of the dishonest steward (Luke 16: 1–8). Ask that each person formulate a question about the parable. After a few minutes each person can raise the question that occurs to him as he looks at the parable. Let other persons respond to the question as they interpret the parable. In a small group (about eight) go around the entire group in this way. If the group is large, select about four people to pose their questions and then ask whether there are any other questions that are different from the ones that have been presented. The leader may summarize, drawing the elements of the discussion together.

2. If there are more than eight present, divide into buzz groups of five or six persons each and assign half the parable of the costly tower and the other half the parable of the rash king. Ask each group to discuss its parable and its application for six to ten minutes and then to report one major idea. It would be very helpful if the questions given below were written on a blackboard or newsprint chart so that the buzz groups could see them. One group could deal primarily with question *a*, another with question *b*, and a third with question *c*, and a fourth with question *d*.

The value of this technique, which at first may seem to be unnecessary effort and bother, is that it gets a much freer discussion with many more persons being able to participate. Ideas are richer, learning includes more active thought, and persons feel freer as they come to know one another's inner thoughts better. It does much to build group spirit, respect, and discussion of ideas, and lifts exchange of ideas above the level of pleasantries.

If your group is small, or if the suggested plan is not feasible, read together the two parables. They are excellent for raising questions concerning our sense of religious obedience and responsibility. They point up the tragedy of words that come easily and without the willingness to follow through and pay the cost. It would be better never to begin being disciples than to begin without the readiness to pay the price of following through. The following questions, as well as those that come from the group, can be used for discussion.

a What do the parables suggest about the conditions of discipleship?

b We often hear the advice that a man should do what makes him happy. How does this compare with the Christian concept of sacrifice and the cost of discipleship?

c What relevance do these parables have to modern churchmanship and to a Christian life?

d Does the phrase, "religious freedom," lead us to the wrong attitude that religion is free?

CONCLUDING THE SESSION

Close the session by bringing out the significant points of the discussion. Hunter summarizes the two parables with the remark: "In the first parable Jesus says, 'Sit down and reckon whether you can afford to follow me.' In the second he says: 'Sit down and reckon whether you can afford to refuse my demands.'"[2]

ASSIGNMENT

Assignments must be made for session three if optional session two is to be omitted. The group may study "The Willingness to Venture" in the resource book, pp. 75–80, for session three. (Session two covers pp. 69–71, which have already been assigned, but can be reviewed.)

ADDITIONAL RESOURCES

Ask one person to read the exposition of the parable of the talents in *The Interpreter's Bible*. Ask that he compare the commentary on the account in Matthew 25: 14–30 with that in Luke 19: 11–17.

the price
of gaining the kingdom

The person, who in decisiveness wills to be
and to remain loyal to the Good, can find time
for all possible things. No, he
cannot do that. But neither does he
need to do that, for he wills only
one thing, and just on that account he will
not have to do all possible things, and so
he finds ample time for the Good.   —Kierkegaard [1]

PURPOSE OF THIS SESSION

The parables of the hidden treasure (Matthew 13: 44) and the pearl of great price (Matthew 13: 45–46) also deal with the demands of discipleship. They do not deal with the cost of discipleship or the ability to carry through so much as they deal with the demand for complete surrender that discipleship lays on those who would heed the call, "Follow me." In this session we strive to discover the relevance of these companion parables for the follower of Jesus.

BEGINNING THE SESSION

Here are two very brief but dramatic parables that can be treated as a pair. Read them and discuss their implications.

DEVELOPING THE SESSION

Select from the following suggestions those that seem significant for the purpose of this session.

*An optional session.

PETER SCHLAIFER

1. Observe the similarities between the two parables involved in this discussion. Are there any differences? Why do so many parables seem to come in pairs?

2. Use the parables to raise questions about the meaning of discipleship today. Do some of us take discipleship too much for granted? What does the demand which these parables stress mean in terms of a man's devotion to his job, his family, and his church? Do these have to be "sold" in order to purchase the "pearl of great price?"

3. How does a person surrender himself, his family, or his business? Remember that in the invitation to the banquet (marriage feast) it was business and family that kept the man from eating "bread in the kingdom of God."

4. Can a Christian ever get done doing the good that he is supposed to? A non-church woman criticized Christians to her neighbor by saying: "Christians always seem to be driven to want to do more. They don't ever seem to have any ease. They are disturbed people." What do you think about this description of Christians? Read the quotation under "Thought for the Leader," and ask the group whether that throws any light on the question raised by the woman's criticism of Christians. About whom does Kierkegaard say, "He will not have to do all possible things, and so finds ample time for the good?"

5. Discuss the concept of joy in the parable of the hidden treasure. What is the difference between joy and happiness? Does Christian discipleship promise joy or happiness —or both? Should a person seek happiness? Is it a worthy goal in life to do the things that make you happy, or is this selfishness?

6. Let someone try to summarize the gist of the discussion in order that the significant ideas that have recurred are pointed up in the conclusion.

ASSIGNMENT

The assignment for session three was given at the conclusion of session one, and may be found there. Session three is based on the parable of the talents (Matthew 25: 14–30 and Luke 19: 12–28).

session 3

the willingness to venture

Lead on, O King eternal!
The day of march has come;
Henceforth in fields of conquest
Thy tents shall be our home.
Through days of preparation
Thy grace has made us strong,
And now, O King eternal,
We lift our battle song.

—Ernest W. Shurtleff

Thy grace has made us strong.

PURPOSE OF THIS SESSION

The parable of the talents (Matthew 25: 14–30 and Luke 19: 11–27) is a very familiar but difficult parable. Its original meaning and form is obscured by two versions reported in Matthew and Luke that developed in the early church's usage and transmission of the parable. This session endeavors to get at the heart of the meaning of the parable, as well as to understand some of the reasons for the divergent traditions of the details.

BEGINNING THE SESSION

Pages 75–80, in the resource book, "The Willingness to Venture," are a discussion of the two forms in which the parable occurs (Matthew 25: 14–30 and Luke 19: 11–27). Begin by comparing the two forms in detail. Using this section of the resource book, try to understand something of the process by which the variations have occurred. A specific point for interesting observation can be the varying amounts of money entrusted and the varying number of people in each of the forms of the parable. Any persons who have done additional reading can contribute to the general progress of the discussion.

If unanswerable questions are raised, ask the person who asked the question to look up the answer. You can offer help by being able to refer to books that deal with the question. It is also possible that the person could go to the pastor or other church members for the answer to certain questions. Research projects, which are usually reported on at the beginning of the next session, provide both a valuable experience for the seeker and a review of the discussion and thought of the previous session.

DEVELOPING THE SESSION

Use the filmstrip for this course, *Five Parables of Jesus*, for a visual presentation of the parable of the talents. Let the filmstrip tell the story of the parable. Following the presentation engage in a discussion of the impact the filmstrip makes in presenting the message of the parable. How does the visual form affect the viewer compared with the reading of the parable? To what degree can such a medium suggest the true interpretation of a parable, or obscure it? Does the way the filmstrip emphasizes the words of the parable create a different impression from that which you received in reading it?

After the discussion of the parable as the filmstrip helps to visualize it, suggest applications of the parable to our modern day. Notice how the situation to which it is addressed varies in the gospels. Observe its context in Matthew. This again is a good parable to carry in the mind through the week and to contemplate in relation to the events that occur.

Raise the following quotation from the resource book for discussion. "You are willing to do business with foreigners and unclean people, but you are unwilling to trade the faith with them, assuming that it is for yourselves alone. You store it like money put in a sock." (Page 80.)

ASSIGNMENT

The reading assignment is pp. 80–83 in the resource book. Ask each person to read Matthew 13: 1–23, Mark 4: 1–20, or Luke 8: 4–15, and to consider whether this parable ought to be named the *sower* or the *soils*.

ADDITIONAL RESOURCES

Eugene Burnard's "The Talents," appears on p. 653 of *Christ and the Fine Arts*. An interpretation of the picture is on p. 618. The picture can provide a good point of discussion for the parable. The interpretation offers idleness and sloth as the sin of the one-talent man. Does the group accept this as an adequate statement of the problem of the parable? Does this interpretation agree with that offered in the resource book? Does the group feel that the picture presents the idea suggested in the interpretation?

Ask three people to read different interpretations of the parable of the sower. Books that might be suggested include Hunter, *Interpreting the Parables, The Interpreter's Bible,* and any other available book that the group has found useful and true to the meaning of the parables.

PETER SCHLAIFER

session 4

confidence
  in God's word

Go forth to sow the living seed;
    Seek not earth's praise, nor dread its blame;
Nor labors fear, nor trials heed;
    Go forth to conquer in his name.

Lo, I am with you, saith the Lord,
    My grace your spirit shall sustain;
Strong is my arm, and sure my word;
    My servants shall not toil in vain.

PURPOSE OF THIS SESSION

The parable of the sower (Matthew 13: 1–23; Mark 4: 1–20; and Luke 8: 4–15) has been interpreted as an explanation for the various kinds of reception that the gospel will receive in the world, and also as a parable that gives confidence in the inevitable harvest that proclaiming the gospel brings. What is involved in each interpretation that seems to catch the spirit of the parable? As it deals with proclaiming the gospel, the parable presents another aspect of the responsibility of the disciple.

BEGINNING THE SESSION

Confront the group with one or all of the following discussion questions about the parable of the sower.

1. Do we tend to identify ourselves with the sower or with the different kinds of soils? Most of us probably are conditioned to think of ourselves in terms of the kind of soil: are we good soil for receiving God's word or does it spring up and die? The parable has been used for upbraiding one another religiously and morally. Is it legitimate for us as disciples to see ourselves in terms of the sower and to identify with him? If so, what change takes place in the parable?

2. Does reading this parable give you the feeling of confidence or of futility?

3. Is this a parable of sowing or of soils? Does the allegorical interpretation seem to fit the central meaning of the parable?

DEVELOPING THE SESSION

Turn attention to the interpretation of this parable in the resource book, pp. 80–83. Allow time for discussion of the emphasis given in this interpretation.

Show the filmstrip presentation of the parable of the sower and follow it with a discussion of the interpretation as the filmstrip enlightens it. Does the filmstrip add any new facets to the understanding of the parable that did not come out in the discussion of it?

III—4

If application of the parable to Christian disciples has not come out in the previous discussion, pursue the question of application to the life of the modern church, and the view of discipleship that it assumes. Mark 4: 21–25 can also be included in the discussion of the application, because this provides the context for perceiving the meaning of the parable. It is included in the discussion in the resource book.

CONCLUDING THE SESSION

Summarize the session by asking several persons to give one significant point or idea which they believe came out of the session.

REVIEW AND RECOLLECTION

Now that we have come to the end of the section on entering the kingdom or the demand of discipleship, this would be a good time to reserve the last fifteen minutes for returning the statements that the group wrote at the beginning of the course on the meaning of the kingdom of God (session four of Unit I), in order that they can look at their own statements. Discuss whether you would now state the meaning of the kingdom in the same way. Have certain emphases changed in your minds, or would you begin from an entirely different perspective?

ASSIGNMENT

Study chapter 8, pages 85–99 in the resource book, *Exploring the Parables.*

a God-centered life

Our dilemma at the moment is not unlike that of
the sorcerer's apprentice. As Goethe tells the
story, the apprentice had observed how
his master made difficult tasks easy
and disagreeable chores pleasant
by simply uttering a few magic words.
When one day the apprentice was told to carry
water from the spring
for the master's bath,
he spied a broom in the corner of the room,
and availing himself of the few
magic words that he knew,
he commanded the broom to take the buckets and
bring in the water. Unfortunately his joy soon
turned to frenzy. In spite of his protestations, the
broom kept carrying in water and yet more water.
What to do? Soon the room as well as the tub was
filled to overflowing.
Threatened to be swept to his death by the flood
his magic had released, the apprentice was heard
to cry when the master magician appeared upon
the scene in the nick of time, "The spirits which I
invoked, they will not leave me now."

—F. W. Schroeder[1]

PETER SCHLAIFER

PURPOSE OF THIS SESSION

The unjust judge (Luke 18: 1–8) is a seldom used but striking parable that makes its message vivid by means of an unusual contrast. No other parable reveals more clearly that the parables as a form of teaching are not stories that present a moral example. This session is concerned with understanding man's dependence upon God. It consists of a study of the parable of the unjust judge, and the study of as many of the following parables on this subject as time will allow you to consider: the parables of the Pharisee and the publican (Luke 18: 9–14), the persistent friend (Luke 11: 5–8), the two debtors (Luke 7: 36–50), and the unclean spirit (Matthew 12: 43–45 and Luke 11: 24–26).

BEGINNING THE SESSION

Discuss the novel technique of the parable of the unjust judge (Luke 18:1–8): how the judge is described as an undesirable character, and yet is the one to whom God is likened in a certain way. Consider the emphasis which the parable places on persistence. What application does the group see for this attribute in man's approach to God? Does it have the meaning of "Keep trying"?

DEVELOPING THE SESSION

Choose from the following suggestions for discussion.

1. In one way or another this parable suggests man's dependence upon God. Your discussion might deal with various aspects of dependence and how it is acknowledged or how men refuse to acknowledge it. How are prayer and persistent seeking both acknowledgments of dependence?

2. Read the "Thought for the Leader" given in session one of Unit III and discuss the meaning of the poem in relation to the parable of the unjust judge.

3. Discuss the story of the unclean spirit (Matthew 12: 43–45 and Luke 11: 24–26). This is a very interesting and revealing narrative about what it means to live for God. Discuss how this message goes against so much of the common definition of what it is to be religious: not to be bad in any way.

4. The parable of the Pharisee and the publican (resource book pp. 87–88) is relevant to this whole subject. Here is another form of the expression of dependence upon God. Dependence means giving up trust in one's own goodness and living for God, conscious that life depends upon his goodness.

In connection with the discussion of the parable of the Pharisee and the publican, what modern application of the parable is given in the following poem by Alice Meynell called "The Newer Vainglory"?

> Two men went up to pray; and one gave thanks,
>   Not with himself—aloud,
> With proclamation, calling on the ranks
>   Of an attentive crowd.
>
> "Thank God, I clap not my own humble breast,
>   But other ruffians' backs,
> Imputing crime—such is my tolerant haste—
>   To any man that lacks.
>
> "For I am tolerant, generous, keep no rules,
>   And the age honours me.
> Thank God, I am not as these rigid fools,
>   Even as this Pharisee." [2]

The poem suggests that self-righteousness takes many non-religious forms today as people think they are better than the Pharisee.

David Noss tells the story of the church school teacher who after teaching the parable of the Pharisee and the publican, stressing the Pharisee's false sense of superiority, went on to say in concluding the session, "Come let us pray and thank God that we are not like that Pharisee." A contemporary group will inevitably be amused at this. Ask them why they expressed amusement. Let them discuss why they smiled. Is it that *we feel superior* to that Pharisaical church school teacher? What light does all this throw on the reality of the problem with which the parable deals?

5. Look at the parable of the two debtors (Luke 7: 36–50) and its context. Here is a parable in its original setting, and we see how Jesus used it in relation to a particular Pharisee,

Simon. Discuss Luke 7: 47. Do people who have a strict sense of justice and moral discipline find it difficult to forgive others who fail to live up to their moral standards? To what degree is love related to knowing one's own needs? Does this relate to the parable of the Pharisee and the publican? (Luke 18: 9–14.)

SUMMARIZING THE SESSION

Because of the widely divergent parables treated, let someone summarize what seems to be the common thread that runs through the whole session, and how each of these parables contributes to it in a specific way. What are the various ways in which dependence upon God can be expressed? Or denied?

ASSIGNMENT

The next session is an optional one (III–6) and is based on the parables of the rich fool (Luke 12: 16–21) and that which defiles (Mark 7: 14–23). If you plan to omit that session, III–7 is based on the parable of the good Samaritan (Luke 10: 29–37). In either case ask everyone to study pp. 91–99 of the resource book.

ADDITIONAL RESOURCES

If you have someone interested in scholarly opinions, have him study the exegesis and exposition in *The Interpreter's Bible* on Luke 16: 9–13. This would be done only if session III–6 is to be used.

It would enhance the next session if you were to begin it with a thought-provoking description of Flavia in *A Serious Call to a Devout and Holy Life*, by William Law. If this book is not in your church library consult your minister or the public library. It is available in a complete and an abridged edition by Westminster Press. The abridged edition is designed for lay discussion groups. The description of Flavia is in chapter VII, pp. 67–70 of the complete edition, and pp. 48–51 of the abridged edition.

a right
use of things

If it be asked why religion does not get
possession of their hearts, the reason is this;
it is not because they live in gross sins,
or debaucheries,
for their regard to religion preserves them
from such disorders; but it is because
their hearts are constantly employed,
perverted, and kept in a wrong state by the indis-
creet use of such things as are lawful to be used.
   The use and enjoyment of their estate is lawful, and therefore it never
comes into their heads to imagine
any great danger from that quarter.
They never reflect, that there is a vain and
impudent use of their estate, which,
though it does not destroy like gross sins,
yet so disorders the heart, and supports it in
such sensuality and dulness,
such pride and vanity, as makes it incapable
of receiving the life and spirit of piety.

—William Law[1]

*An optional session.

PURPOSE OF THIS SESSION

This session deals with some of the things that define the relation of man to the material world and to his neighbor. The previous session dealt with man's relation to God. Here we seek to extend the meaning of the relationship that stems from that basic one. You will notice that a prominent parable like that of the good Samaritan has been omitted from this session in order to receive more thorough treatment later. It can certainly be referred to in this session, but its treatment later will reinforce the central aspect of the basic teaching already stressed in this session. One reason for its omission here is that instead of being a metaphorical story it falls into the class of illustrative stories or story examples showing the meaning of the word *neighbor*. It does not fit the usual definition of a parable.

BEGINNING THE SESSION

Turn to the parable of the rich fool in Luke 12:16–21, and follow in Bibles while someone reads the parable aloud. Let the group express its observations on this parable. Did the discussion throw any new significance upon the parable itself?

DEVELOPING THE SESSION

If someone has read the description William Law gives of Flavia in *A Serious Call to a Devout and Holy Life,* have him report. Discuss this portrait. In general it reflects the meaning of the quotation given in the thought for the leader. After the discussion of the portrait of Flavia, read the thought for the leader, as well as the following quotation which reflects the same point.

"Now it is for want of religious exactness in the use of these innocent and lawful things, that religion cannot get possession of our hearts. And it is in the right and prudent management of ourselves, as to these things, that all the art of holy living chiefly consists." [2]

What is the basic attitude and use that a man should make of the things of the world? You will notice that according to William Law it is innocent things wrongly used that are the most deceptive temptations.

1. Recall some of the statements of the sermon on the mount referred to in the resource book that also deal with the crucial problem of man's use of material things. Interesting and arresting statements on the same problem are found in Luke 16: 9–13. Each of these verses, because of its location after the parable, seems to reflect a different approach to the parable when connected to it. Read the verses. If someone has prepared an assignment on them, receive his report. This can be the stimulus for discussion. Because they all deal in some way with the issue of wealth, they seem to be a group of miscellaneous sayings that have been collected here at the end of this parable. Have the group attempt to interpret each of these verses. The resource book may also be of help.

2. Man's relationship to things expressed in the parable of the rich fool (Luke 12: 16–21) might be summed up in the words of J. H. Jowett, reported by F. W. Schroeder. Let the group hear these words and reflect upon them. "In a memorable sermon entitled 'Thirsting for the Springs,' found in the book by the same title, the late J. H. Jowett, one of the great preachers of all times, observed: 'God has made the grass very juicy for the kine, but the juices of the grass do not make the kine independent of the waterbrooks. . . . And God has made some things very juicy for his children, in order that the juiciness itself might minister to our delight and growth. . . . But even in these luxurious pastures the soul thirsts for the springs.'" [3]

3. Instead of concentrating on man's relationship to material things as has been done in this session, it would also be possible to concentrate on man's relationship with his neighbor. The group could concentrate on the application of the parable of the unforgiving servant (Matthew 18: 23–35). Is forgiveness always really possible in our world? Was it easier to forgive in ancient times, when a man knew personally all of the people he dealt with, than now when so many of our dealings are impersonal? In what way is our forgiving related to God's forgiveness?

4. A section of the chapter deals with man's right understanding of himself as a child of God. It can be said that until a man has a right view and relation of himself, he will always be unable to relate himself rightly to others. Your group might be asked to illustrate this statement.

The following quotation might become the basis for discussion. In *Far From Home*, F. W. Schroeder writes:

"Some years ago Walter Lippmann gave a telling account of the dilemma of the liberated in his *Preface to Morals*. He wrote of brave and brilliant atheists who had defied God, and had become very nervous; of women who had emancipated themselves from the tyranny of homes and husbands and were 'enduring liberty as interior decorators' with the intermittent help of psychoanalysts; of young men and women world-weary at twenty-two. All these, he declared, ought to be very happy, for were they not free to make their own lives?" [4]

SUGGESTIONS FOR USING THE ABOVE IDEAS

Because of the variety of suggestions made above it is suggested that the group be divided into subgroups of five to eight persons, or into four subgroups, and that each of the groups be given one of the suggestions for its own study. To facilitate the discussion in each of the subgroups the leader should have prepared typewritten cards or sheets with the subject, the quotations, or the questions that each of the subgroups is to discuss. At the conclusion of this period of subgroup discussion, reports can be made to the whole group in the final ten minutes of the session. Each report can give the problem that the subgroup tackled and the ideas that came forth in the discussion of it.

If the group is of such a size that it can form only two or three subgroups of five or six persons each, you can choose those suggestions that seem most significant and interesting from your knowledge of the group. In larger groups where more than four subgroups result, several subgroups can discuss the same question and compare their ideas in the reporting session. If one of the suggestions does not seem significant, it can be omitted.

ASSIGNMENT

Ask the group to reread and study pp. 96–99 in the resource book. The next session will be based on the parable of the good Samaritan (Luke 10: 29–37).

session 7

go thou and
do likewise

I know the road to Jericho,
    It's in a part of town
That's full of factories and filth
    I've seen the folks go down.

Small folk with roses in their cheeks
    And starlight in their eyes;
And seen them fall among the thieves,
    And heard their helpless cries.

The priests and Levites speeding by
    Read of the latest crimes
In headlines spread in black and red
    Across *The Evening Times*.
How hard for those in limousines
    To heal the heart of man!
It was a slow-paced ass that bore
    The Good Samaritan.

—Edwin McNeill Poteat [1]

PURPOSE OF THIS SESSION

These parables form a unique group in that they are really narratives that give examples of behavior. In this respect they are very much like the story the prophet Nathan told to David. Our purpose in this session is to study one of them—the parable of the good Samaritan—and its implication for our lives.

BEGINNING THE SESSION

The resource book discusses in detail the lawyer's attitude in questioning Jesus and the way in which Jesus treats his question. Discuss this, especially noting how Jesus refuses to answer questions based on false premises and shifts the ground of the question before he replies.

Also observe that in the lawyer's second question, although the ground was shifted, he was defending himself instead of being willing to grow. What does the group think of the statements in the resource book: "Talk of religion is easily confused with serving God. . . . Religious discussion groups can become an escape from meeting the judgment of God face to face. Pious questions, the desire to more secure viewpoints, the urge to make our definitions accurate, might only be a way to avoid the necessity for action" (p. 98).

Are there times when we ask questions from wrong motives and in wrong terms that really should not be answered? Can the group think of questions which we ask that are really not attempt to grow in understanding?

After the discussion of the spirit and motive in questioning, and how Jesus deals with these, use the filmstrip of the story of the good Samaritan to introduce the parable. The filmstrip presents the biblical text, but the group will want to have Bibles open for reference during the discussion that follows.

The remaining part of the session can use some of the alternatives suggested below.

1. What is involved in the fact that Jesus refuses to discuss the definition of "Who is my neighbor?" but rather discusses what the neighborly man is?

2. Let the group hear the poem which is used in the "Thought for the Leader." After its reading, discuss it as an application of the story of the good Samaritan. Members of the group can expand on other ways in which we are the priest and the levite who pass by on the other side.

3. Arrange for some activity or action that the group can engage in to express a neighborly concern. Certainly this ought to include some fellowship with people who are usually overlooked.

4. Ivan in *The Brothers Karamazov* by Dostoevski makes the comment, "I could never understand how one can love one's neighbor. It's just one's neighbors, to my mind, that one can't love, though one might love those at a distance." [2]

5. This parable has given us such everyday expressions as "passing by on the other side," and "playing the good Samaritan." Can the group think of other everyday expressions which we use that come from the parables? What does usage suggest about the parables? Does use of these expressions indicate that we are making a modern application of the parable? (Other common expressions include: "gathering them from the highways and byways," "playing the Pharisee," "counting the cost," "bearing the burden of the day," "the eleventh hour," "the leaven and the lump.")

ASSIGNMENTS

Ask that everyone reread and study pp. 91–99 in the resource book. The last session in this unit will deal with the parable of the unworthy servant (Luke 17: 7–10).

ADDITIONAL RESOURCES

"The Good Samaritan" by Van Gogh is found in a black and write print in *The Church and the Fine Arts*, together with a picture interpretation, p. 518. The class might find it significant to view the picture, or it might be used as a focus for a brief worship emphasis. Rembrandt also has a painting entitled, "The Good Samaritan."

"The Secret Life of the Good Samaritan," the title story of the book by Robert John Versteeg, is an excellent additional resource on this parable.

self-discipline

Cheap grace means grace sold on the market like cheapjack's wares. The sacraments, the forgiveness of sin and the consolations of religion are thrown away at cut prices. Grace is represented as the Church's inexhaustible treasury, from which she showers blessings with generous hands, without asking questions or fixing limits. . . .

Instead of following Christ, let the Christian enjoy the consolations of his grace! That is what we mean by cheap grace, the grace which amounts to the justification of sin without the justification of the repentant sinner who departs from sin and from whom sin departs. Cheap grace is not the kind of forgiveness of sin which frees us from the toils of sin. Cheap grace is the grace we bestow upon ourselves.

Cheap grace is the preaching of forgiveness without requiring repentance, baptism without church discipline, Communion without confession, absolution without personal confession. Cheap grace is grace without discipleship, grace without the Cross, grace without Jesus Christ, living and incarnate.

Costly grace is the treasure hidden in the field; for the sake of it a man will gladly go and sell all that he has. It is the pearl of great price to buy for which the merchant will sell all his goods. It is the kingly role of Christ, for whose sake a man will pluck out the eye which causes him to stumble, it is the call of Jesus Christ at which the disciple leaves his nets and follows him.

Such grace is *costly* because it calls us to follow, and it is *grace* because it calls us to follow *Jesus Christ*. It is costly because it costs a man his life, and it is grace because it gives a man the only true life. It is costly because it condemns sin, and grace because it justifies the sinner.

—Bonhoeffer[1]

PURPOSE OF THIS SESSION

One of the most suggestive parables is little empha-
sized in our contemporary church. Yet its message seems
to sum up the meaning of the life of any Christian disciple.
Perhaps it is neglected because it emphasizes not the free
character of God's love, but the obligation that God's grace
places upon us. The parable of the unworthy servant
(Luke 17: 7–10) is studied here as a kind of summary of
this whole unit entitled "The Life of Discipleship." It por-
trays the basic spirit of the follower of Christ.

BEGINNING THE SESSION

Ask persons to suggest what the word *self-discipline*
means to them. Once the discussion is under way it might
be pointed out that the word *disciple* is the root of the
word *discipline.* What is the inevitable connection between
the two that makes the word *discipline* merely the development of the word *disciple?* In the light of the meaning of
disciple that has been brought out in previous sessions, and
the fact that a disciple is one committed to God, or who
lives a God-centered life, what significance does this have
for the word *discipline?* The most crucial question, and the
one which is the climax for such a discussion is: What is
the motivation for self-discipline, especially in the light of
its relation to the word *disciple?*

DEVELOPING THE SESSION

Read the parable of the unworthy servant (Luke 17:
7–10). What is the attitude the servant takes toward that
which he has already done? Does he expect praise for it?
What is the reward for having done your job? This narrative
has unlimited application as we think of its relation to our
understanding of the meaning and motive of Christian discipleship.

1. Instead of thinking of our responsibilities to God in the
church as our duty, do we not think of them as voluntary
and expect to be thanked for them? Are we not insulted if
no one compliments us for the good we have done? How
many times have we said, "I won't do that anymore if no
one appreciates it"? But if we have only done what was

demanded, it puts an entirely different light on things. All we can say is, "We have only done our duty."

2. Discuss the following questions. Has the phrase "freedom of religion" in our society led to misconceptions in certain areas of thought? Has it carried the overtone that religion was *free:* without obligation or cost? Have Protestants understood the meaning of the word *freedom* when applied to their faith, or has it meant a loss of the sense of obligation or duty?

3. Discuss the source of the concept of duty. What gives man a sense of duty? The parable itself provides an insight into the source of duty when it bases it on the fact that the master has expectations of the servant. It is only when we know who our master is and that he has expectations of us that we recognize "we are unworthy servants; we have only done what was our duty" (Luke 17: 10).

4. How does the idea of only having done your duty affect the concept of a religion of reward-seeking or profit? What effect does it have on seeking the reward of heaven? What about perfect attendance awards?

5. How does the meaning of discipleship and discipline keep the Christian from the sense of smugness and self-satisfaction that characterized some Pharisees? Compare Luke 22:25–27 where the role of the servant is contrasted with that of profitable lords.

6. What light does this whole discussion throw on the parable in Luke 14:7–10?

ASSIGNMENT

Ask that everyone study chapter nine of the resource book, especially the first part, "God and the Sinner."

ASSIGNMENT IN RELATION TO CONCLUDING THE COURSE

In preparation for a final summary and review of this course, have several persons prepare a chart which gives the outline of the resource book and lists the parables that have been studied under each of the sections of the chart. This will provide a vivid visual summary of all the parables that have been studied, and of the subjects under which they have been considered.

Let several other persons in the group work out charts that give different groupings of the parables. The list of parables depends upon one's definition of a parable; especially is this manifest in the case of parables that approach the narrowest portion of the dividing line between parables and non-parables.

Two listings of parables are included in this coursebook (pp. 126 and 127).

All of these charts are to be completed for the last session of this course. When the charts are presented they should be accompanied by reasons as to why the parables are grouped as they are. This will also provide a quick review of the parables and their general subjects, while freeing them from any slavish listing or grouping.

If it is possible after the last session to get one or both of the additional charts duplicated, so that they can be handed out to the members of the group, it will provide them with a summary of the course and an easy means of finding any parable to which they wish to refer at future times.

ADDITIONAL RESOURCES

If *Parables of Crisis*, by Edwin McNeill Poteat, is available, ask someone to read its account of the parable of the prodigal son.

The stories entitled "The Prodigals" and "The Sheep" in *The Secret Life of the Good Samaritan* by Robert John Versteeg are excellent additional resources for the next session.

UNIT IV

the way of God with man

The rule of God and the responsibilities it lays upon men impresses us with some of the contrasts between God's way and man's. Unit IV deals with general parables about God's relationship with man.

Session one contrasts God's rejoicing over regaining the lost while the elder brother is grudgingly resentful.

Session two deals with the ways that man hopes to deal with and motivate his fellow man. It contrasts them with God's. God does his work in ways that contrast with man's appeal to the miraculous.

Finally, God's way of dealing with man is in Jesus Christ. He is the giver of the parables, but more than this he mediates the power of God in his own person so that history and even the parables take on an authority and power that mere words or teaching could never possess. This is the theme of session three, the conclusion of the course.

PETER SCHLAIFER

session 1

God and the sinner

> Who sees a spire against the sky
> Shall find, at last, the sign
> Of all he sought—nor ever found—
> In land of husks and swine.
> Who enters there and kneels, shall know
> That place no hands can build
> Where man, the prodigal, is Home,
> His soul's long hunger filled.

—Leslie Savage Clark [1]

PURPOSE OF THIS SESSION

In this session we will survey the parables in Luke 15 that deal with the ways and purposes of God in his relationship with man. Three parables are related to each other and are dealt with in this session: the lost sheep (Matthew 18: 12–14; Luke 15: 3–7); the lost coin (Luke 15: 8–10); and the prodigal son (Luke 15: 11–32). In one way or another they contrast the ways of God with the ways of man.

BEGINNING THE SESSION

There is an abundance of material available for use in this session, and therefore the teaching possibilities.are many.

1. Begin by using the portion of the filmstrip that is about the parable of the lost sheep, if it was not used in session three of Unit I. Follow it with a discussion of the meaning and the feeling that the filmstrip arouses.

2. Or begin the session by using the picture, "The Lost Sheep," in Maus, *Christ and the Fine Arts,* p. 203. There might be a larger colored copy of this picture somewhere in the church. Look at this picture and then discuss the meaning and feeling that one gets from seeing it. After this discussion has proceeded, let one person who is prepared tell the interpretation of the picture as given in Maus, pp. 204–205. After this recollect how the audience to which a parable is addressed determines something of its central meaning. Remember that the parable in the gospel of Luke is told not to console the distressed about how God will always love them, but it is told against those who are critical of Jesus eating with tax collectors and sinners. Discuss the question as to whether the picture has preserved this context or whether it left the original context behind and generalized the parable so that a man today would not see the implied criticism of those who objected to the company which Jesus kept.

3. Omit the parable of the lost sheep, since it was treated earlier, and discuss briefly the parable of the lost coin. Compare it with the lost sheep. Notice the emphasis that falls on the joy of the father.

DEVELOPING THE SESSION

Proceed to the discussion of the parable of the prodigal son. After the parable has been read, observe the obvious difference between this and the preceding parables. The presentation in the resource book will be an aid here. Too frequently this parable has been interpreted as being similar to the other two, which means that the elder brother has been omitted. Observe that *the elder brother is the point of this story,* because his attitude toward the prodigal is contrasted with that of the father. This parable is not a description of the father, but a contrast between him and the elder brother. The confusion results from the fact that the context of the parable as being told against those who criticize Jesus' associations with sinners is forgotten. Certainly it would be harder to think of Jesus as someone who is sentimental, meekly forgiving, and spineless if we remembered the context in which these three parables on seeking the lost are told. They carry a sharp rebuke within them. Recollecting this fact also ought to keep us from thinking too sentimentally of God in the parable of the prodigal son. The father in the story might not utter a rebuke, but the parable itself is a rebuke.

Urge the group to keep the context in mind as they discuss the parable. What is the sin of the elder brother? Ask members of the group to put themselves in the place of the elder brother and imagine his feelings. Ask them to expand his arguments and his defense. Does it sound modern in any way? Or ask two people to put themselves into the characters of the elder brother and the father, and to conduct their argument or defense with each other concerning the elder brother's insult. This role-play can make vivid the feelings and point of view of each character and provide a good basis for discussion. After they have played the part the participants can share what it meant to be in their particular situation.

Is not the elder brother justified in his insult? Is it fair to reward the prodigal and to take the elder brother for granted? Or is the elder brother really being taken for granted? This parable provides a marvelous opportunity for discovering what it means for man to be in relationship with God and with one's fellow man. In what sense might the elder brother's sin be his individualism in which he has lost the sense of family unity?

E. M. Poteat, in this treatment of this parable in his book *Parables of Crisis*, identifies three prodigals—the third being the prodigal father who spoils his elder son and nullifies the fruits of the younger son's repentance with a cheap concept of forgiveness. His gift of restored status is purely material and the same kind of property status that he had lost: the ring, the robe, and roast veal. Discuss this shocking idea about the parable. It at least keeps us from identifying the father in the story with God too easily. Nevertheless, is this interpretation relevant to the Bible text as written? What interpretations have you been able to find in other commentaries? Poteat feels that we have missed the point of the parable by making it a picture of salvation where it was not so intended.

SUMMARIZING THE SESSION

Show the filmstrip story of the parable of the prodigal son as a summary of the session. You should have previewed it to see how it meets the questions raised in the session plan. Allow the filmstrip to tell its own story as a summary, and do not follow it with any formal discussion. Perhaps some will want to talk informally about it after the session has ended.

ASSIGNMENT

The reading assignment is the section entitled "God's Miracles" in the last part of chapter nine in the resource book. Ask the group to contemplate as they read this assignment what relevance the message of the parable of the rich man and Lazarus (Luke 16:19–31) might have in understanding the resurrection of Jesus.

ADDITIONAL RESOURCES

"The Lost Sheep," by Alfred Soord, in Maus, *Christ and the Fine Arts*, and the picture interpretation on pp. 204–5.

E. M. Poteat, *Parables of Crisis*, New York, Harper and Row, 1950, pp. 134–150.

F. W. Schroeder, *Far From Home*, Philadelphia, Christian Education Press, 1961.

Ask two members to read about the parable of the rich man and Lazarus in appropriate books such as *The Interpreter's Bible* in order to explain the unusual terms and get the important background data. What is meant, for example, by such terms as "Moses and the prophets" and "Abraham's bosom"?

session 2

God's miracles

How is it proved?
It isn't proved, you fool! It can't be proved.
How can you prove a victory before
It's won? How can you prove a man who leads
To be a leader worth the following,
Unless you follow to the death, and out
Beyond mere death, which is not anything
But Satan's lie upon eternal life?
Well—God's my leader, and I hold that He
Is good, and strong enough to work His plan
And purpose out to its appointed end.

—G. A. Studdert-Kennedy *

PURPOSE OF THIS SESSION

The basic subject of the parable of the rich man and Lazarus (Luke 16: 19–31) deals with fear and reward as motives for becoming religious. This parable suggests that neither the threat of punishment nor the hope of reward will motivate men. They cannot be scared or bribed into the kingdom.

This session also includes a teaching of Jesus that raises implications for understanding the resurrection from the dead. Mark 12: 18–27 indicates Jesus' views on resurrection, but this parable places a meaning on it quite different from that which modern Christians often give to Christ's own resurrection. Therefore, this parable becomes an insight into what Jesus' resurrection must have meant, and a judgment on many modern interpretations of it.

BEGINNING THE SESSION

You might point out that the parable of the rich man and Lazarus, like many others (including those discussed in chapter nine of the resource book and recorded in Luke 15), contrasts the ways of God and the ways of man. Begin by having the group turn to Luke 16: 19–31 and follow in their Bibles while one person reads the parable. If you have had someone do research into the background and meaning of the terms of the parable, encourage the group to ask questions of him. Such terms as "Abraham's bosom" and "Moses and the prophets" should be explained.

DEVELOPING THE SESSION

Discuss the question: What is the central point of the parable? It should be clear that this is not a teaching about heaven and hell, but a parable on the motivation for man's response to God. When the discussion has made this clear, the following questions might be posed.

> What does the rich man expect will motivate his brothers to repentance and a righteous life?
> Why does Abraham reject this concept of motivation as adequate motivation to a righteous life?
> What is the only ground on which man can respond to the will of God?

This parable has innumerable implications that could be discussed at length. The leader can choose those aspects that seem most significant. What light does it throw on the meaning of the resurrection? Could the resurrection be designed to prove the messiahship of Jesus to unbelievers, in view of this parable? To whom were the actual appearances of Jesus made—to those who had crucified him or to those who had in some measure followed him? Is the parable consistent with the actual reports of the resurrection?

If the miracle of the resurrection is not used to prove the faith to outsiders, what meaning does it have? What meaning did it have for the disciples who followed Jesus in his life and now experienced the resurrection? What meaning does the resurrection have for us in the light of Jesus teaching? Compare Mark 12: 18–27.

Discuss the statement in the resource book: "It is only the man of belief who can see the working of God . . . The understanding of the miraculous flows from faith." (page 109.) It is only the man of faith who can know the miracles. In this respect, let the group also hear the poem "The Wager" given under the "Thought for the Leader."

There are other implications of this parable that might also be discussed. One concerns the use of fear as a motive for becoming religious. The rich man in the parable expects his brothers to respond to the motive of fear and the promise of reward. The parable rejects the appeal to threat and reward as adequate means for changing the inner motivation of men. Can the group see any basic reasons for this? On what basis can inner change take place?

SUMMARY

It is important during this session for the leader to summarize the discussion so that the loose ends are tied together and the progression of ideas becomes manifest to all of the participants. The discussion is likely to range far and introduce ideas that challenge some usual ways of thinking.

ASSIGNMENT

Study chapter ten of the resource book, *Exploring the Parables*. It begins on page 111.

session 3

Jesus in the parables

We place Thy sacred name upon our brows;
 Our cycles from Thy natal day we score;
Yet, spite of all our songs and all our vows,
 We thirst and ever thirst to know Thee more.

For Thou art Mystery and Question still;
 Even when we see Thee lifted as a sign
Drawing all men unto that hapless hill
 With the resistless power of Love Divine.

Still Thou art Question—while rings in our ears
 Thine outcry to a world discord-beset:
Have I been with thee all these many years,
 O world—dost thou not know Me even yet?
      —Author unknown *

* From *Christ and the Fine Arts*, Maus (p. 515, revised, enlarged edition). Published by Harper & Brothers, New York 16, New York. Reprinted by special permission of the author-compiler.

CHRIST APPEARS TO THE APOSTLES—Rembrandt

PURPOSE OF THIS SESSION

While we have been discussing the parables of the kingdom, of discipleship, and of God's way with man, we have taken for granted the central figure of the parables— Jesus himself. Although we are aware that he told the parables, in discussing them we often forget Jesus' central place in them because they do not openly talk about him. As in his other sayings, Jesus did not seek first place for himself but sought to glorify God. He saw himself not as the end, but as the one who brought man to the Father. Therefore, he does not talk about himself, but his *life* points to the Father. The parables are not about himself, but about man's relation to God.

It is this humility of Jesus that characterized him as the Son of man and enabled him alone to completely reconcile men to God. But it is this very fact, in a day when we talk about selling ourselves, that means many of us miss the most obvious, although unmentioned fact in the parables: the place of Jesus as the Son.

The purpose of this session is *to discover Jesus Christ as the center of the parables.*

BEGINNING THE SESSION

Express the ideas presented under the purpose of the session. This can serve as an introduction to the discussion of the place of Jesus in the parables.

DEVELOPING THE SESSION

These following points might be brought out. Most of them are made in chapter ten in the resource book.

1. Jesus not only taught the kingdom of God, but men experienced the rule of God when they were near him. They experienced it in his teaching. As presented in the first two chapters of the resource book, his teaching, especially the parable, judged them and demanded decision from them. Jesus did not *inform* them as we think of the purpose of teaching, but he *transformed* them to the reality of God's rule. There was no neutral ground. "He who is not with me is against me," "He who is not against me is with me." Both statements are equally true when seen in this light.

2. There are some teachings of Jesus that present the knowledge that something uniquely new has come into being in his presence. Discuss the sayings listed under "The New and the Old," on page 112 of the resource book.

3. A large part of the gospel ministry of Jesus deals with healing. As in the case of understanding the resurrection, there are a series of parabolic sayings that discuss the meaning of Jesus' healing ministry. Discuss these sayings as they reflect the kingdom of God overcoming evil through the person and activity of Jesus. Here again the sayings reflect the central place of Jesus in bringing the power of the kingdom into reality. The sayings in Mark 3: 20–27 can be compared with those in Matthew 12: 22–30.

4. Finally, Jesus brings in the power of God in his overcoming the barrier of sin. Not only is this made vivid by the setting of the rebuke given to those who accuse him of associating with the undesirable (as indicated in Luke 15), but the resource book attempts to indicate how the very message of the parables on love and forgiveness would be irrelevant if men had come to experience that love and forgiveness in the very person of Jesus. This is a crucial point, and the leader ought to encourage discussion and questions to make sure that it is perfectly clear. Discuss Luke 7: 36–50, the two debtors, as an indication of God's overcoming of sin in Jesus.

SUMMARIZING THE SESSION

Ask for statements from the group on what seems to be the place of Jesus in the faith. How does his life relate even to the issues discussed in many of the other sessions?

CONCLUDING THE COURSE

Let those who have prepared the charts grouping the parables present them and comment on the summary of their contents. Especially let those who have arranged the chart with a different grouping than that used in the resource book explain the grouping and the reason why the various parables are listed as they are. This will serve as an effective summary and free the group from a slavish organization of the parables.

When the review has been completed, discuss some follow-up activities that you might undertake as an outgrowth of this course. No treatment of the teaching of Jesus is complete until we respond to it. This course will not be complete unless the group has felt that it found a new spirit in which to respond to and serve God. Finally, let members of the group who wish to do so, informally share what they feel that they have personally gained from this study of the parables. Such sharing can be a meaningful means of growth in your group.

ADDITIONAL RESOURCES

Bowie, W. R., *The Interpreter's Bible,* vol. VII., pp. 169–171, has a section entitled "What the parables reveal about Jesus." Here he discusses something of Jesus the boy and the man as shown in the parables. While the point of this article is to recover something of the personality of Jesus, and is quite different in intent from this session and the last chapter of the resource book—which seeks to find Jesus' central place in the faith—it nevertheless provides an interesting insight into other aspects of Jesus also revealed in the parables.

ACKNOWLEDGMENTS

UNIT I

SESSION 1

1. From "The Parables" by Walter Russell Bowie. *The Interpreter's Bible,* Volume 7. Copyright 1951 by Pierce and Smith (p. 165). Used by permission of Abingdon Press.

SESSION 2

1. From *The Pilgrim's Progress* by John Bunyan. Rinehart & Co., Inc., 1955. Rinehart Editions (p. 169).
2. From *The Waiting Father* by Helmut Thielicke. Copyright 1959 by John W. Doberstein (pp. 85–86). Used by permission of Harper & Row, Publishers, Incorporated.
3. From *The Gospel Parables in the Light of Their Jewish Background* by W. O. E. Oesterley. Copyright 1936 by The Macmillan Company (pp. 9–10). Used by permission of The Macmillan Company and The Society for Promoting Christian Knowledge.

SESSION 3

1. From *Purity of Heart* by Soren Kierkegaard. Copyright 1959 by Harper & Row, Publishers, Incorporated (pp. 160–161). Used by permission.

SESSION 4

1. *Ibid.,* p. 204.

UNIT II

SESSION 1

1. From "The Vision of Sir Launfal" by James Russell Lowell. *The Complete Poetical Works of James Russell Lowell.* Houghton-Mifflin Company, 1896.
2. Oesterley, *op. cit.,* p. 108.
3. From *Interpreting the Parables* by Archibald M. Hunter. Copyright 1960 by the Student Christian Movement Press, Ltd. (p. 29).

SESSION 2

1. Used by permission of The Proprietors of Hymns Ancient and Modern.

SESSION 3

1. From *A World of Song.* Used by permission of the American Evangelical Lutheran Youth Fellowship.

SESSION 4

1. Kierkegaard, *op. cit.*, p. 161.

SESSION 5

1. From *A Sleep for Prisoners* by Christopher Fry. Copyright 1951 by Christopher Fry (pp. 47–48). Used by permission of Oxford University Press, Inc.

SESSION 6

1. From *Exploring the Parables,* by Eugene S. Wehrli. Copyright 1963 by the United Church Press (p. 102).

UNIT III

SESSION 1

1. From *With All My Heart* by Leslie Savage Clark. Copyright 1957 by Broadman Press. Used by permission.
2. Hunter, *op cit.*, p. 65.

SESSION 2

1. Kierkegaard, *op. cit.*, p. 102.

SESSION 5

1. From *Far From Home* by Frederick W. Schroeder. Copyright 1961 by Christian Education Press (pp. 33–34). Used by permission.
2. From *New Poems–1913* by Alice Meynell. Used by permission of Burns & Oates Ltd.

SESSION 6

1. From *A Serious Call to a Devout and Holy Life* by William Law. The Westminster Press, 1948 (p. 66).
2. *Ibid.*
3. Schroeder, *op. cit.*, p. 61.
4. *Ibid.*, p. 37.

SESSION 7

1. From *Over the Sea, the Sky* by Edwin McNeill Poteat. Copyright 1945 by Harper & Row, Publishers, Incorporated. Used by permission.
2. From *The Brothers Karamazov* by Fedor Dostoevski. Random House, Inc. Modern Library Edition (p. 245).

SESSION 8

1. From *The Cost of Discipleship* by Dietrich Bonhoeffer. Second Edition copyright 1959 by the Student Christian Movement Press, Ltd. (pp. 35–37). Used by permission of the S. C. M. Press, Ltd. and The Macmillan Company.

UNIT IV

SESSION 1

1. Leslie Savage Clark, *op. cit.*

THE LISTING FROM *THE INTERPRETER'S BIBLE* *

In the Gospels of Matthew, Mark, and Luke there are fifty-one passages which may be classed as parables. Listed according to the places of their occurrence, they are as follows.

PARABLES RECORDED IN MATTHEW, MARK, AND LUKE

	MATT.	MARK	LUKE
New patches on old garments	9: 16	2: 21	5: 36
New wine in old wineskins	9: 17	2: 22	5: 37–38
The sower (or the soil)	13: 3–23	4: 2–20	8: 4–15
The mustard seed	13: 31–32	4: 30–32	13: 18–19
The wicked tenants of the vineyard	21: 33–45	12: 1–12	20: 9–19
The budding figtree	24: 32–33	13: 28–29	21: 29–31

PARABLES RECORDED IN MATTHEW AND LUKE

	MATT.	LUKE
The house on the rock and the house on the sand	7: 24–27	6: 47–49
The leaven	13: 33	13: 20–21
The lost sheep	18: 12–14	15: 3–7
The wise steward	24: 45–51	12: 42–48

PARABLES RECORDED IN ONLY ONE GOSPEL

	MATTHEW
The tares	13: 24–30
The hidden treasure	13: 44
The precious pearl	13: 45–46
The dragnet	13: 47–50
The unmerciful servant	18: 23–35
The laborers in the vineyard	20: 1–16
The two sons	21: 28–32
The marriage of the king's son	22: 1–14
The wise and foolish virgins	25: 1–13
The ten talents	25: 14–30
The sheep and the goats	25: 31–46

	MARK
The seed growing silently	4: 26–29
The porter on watch	13: 34–37

	LUKE
The good Samaritan	10: 25–37
The friend at midnight	11: 5–10
The rich fool	12: 16–21
The watchful servants	12: 35–38
The barren fig tree	13: 6–9
The guests who made excuses	14: 16–24
The lost coin	15: 8–10
The prodigal son	15: 11–32
The dishonest steward	16: 1–9
The rich man and Lazarus, the beggar	16: 19–31

* By Walter Russell Bowie in *The Interpreter's Bible*, Volume 7. Copyright 1951 by Pierce and Smith. By permission of Abingdon Press.

The master and the servants	17: 7–10
The persistent widow	18: 1–8
The Pharisee and the publican	18: 9–14
The pounds	19: 11–27

It would be possible to make the foregoing list still longer if every figurative expression of Jesus were included. Among the passages which here have been classed as parables some are exceedingly brief: two or three vivid phrases, the flash of a signal that blazes only for an instant sufficient to show the direction in which thought can follow. Some of them are longer, like the immortal story of the prodigal son, or the unforgettable picture of the good Samaritan.

THE LISTING FROM *INTERPRETING THE PARABLES* *

The following listing of the parables is arranged in accordance with scholars' findings on the source of the parables. It is generally felt that Matthew and Luke drew upon two sources. One of these was the gospel of Mark and the other was a source that has come to be called "Q". This latter document, composed of more than 200 verses, probably ceased to circulate soon after it was incorporated into the Gospels. It is now lost, except for its inclusion in the Gospels. For more detailed information see Volume 7 of *The Interpreter's Bible*, pages 63-65.

MARK

Doctor and Sick (Mark 2: 17)

Wedding Guests (Mark 2: 19 f.)

Patch (Mark 2: 21)

Wineskins (Mark 2: 22)

Divided Realm (Mark 3: 24–26)

Strong Man (Mark 3: 27)

Sower (Mark 4: 3–9)

Lamp and Bushel (Mark 4: 21)

Seed Growing Secretly (Mark 4: 26–29)

Mustard Seed (Mark 4: 30–32)

Savourless Salt (Mark 9: 50)

Wicked Vinedressers (Mark 12:1–9)

Budding Figtree (Mark 13: 28 f.)

Watchman (Mark 13: 34–37)

Q

Blind leading Blind (Luke 6: 39; Matt. 15: 14)

Mote and Beam (Luke 6: 41 f.; Matt. 7: 3–5)

Tree and Fruit (Luke 6: 43–45; Matt. 7: 16–20)

Two Builders (Luke 6: 47–49; Matt. 7: 24–27)

Playing Children (Luke 7: 31 f.; Matt. 11: 16 f.)

Harvest and Labourers (Luke 10: 2; Matt. 9:37 f.)

Asking Son (Luke 11: 11–13; Matt. 7: 9–11)

Divided Realm (Luke 11: 17 f.; Matt. 12: 25 f.)

Strong Man (Luke 11: 21–23; Matt. 12: 29)

Empty House (Luke 11: 24–26; Matt. 12: 43–45)

Lamp and Bushel (Luke 11: 33; Matt. 5: 15)

The Body's Lamp (Luke 11: 34–36; Matt. 6: 22 f.)

Waiting Servants (Luke 12: 35–38)

Burglar (Luke 12: 39 f.; Matt. 24: 43 f.)

Servant in Authority (Luke 12: 42–46; Matt. 24: 45–51)

Weather Signs (Luke 12: 54–56)

Defendant (Luke 12: 57–59; Matt. 5: 25 f.)

Mustard Seed (Luke 13: 18 f.; Matt. 13:31 f.)

Leaven (Luke 13: 21; Matt. 13: 33)

Great Supper (Luke 14: 15–24)

Savourless Salt (Luke 14: 34 f.; Matt. 5: 13)

M

City on Hill (Matt. 5: 14)

Tares (Matt. 13: 24–30)

Hid Treasure (Matt. 13: 44)

Costly Pearl (Matt. 13: 45 f.)

Dragnet (Matt. 13: 47 f.)

Householder (Matt. 13: 52)

Lost Sheep (Matt. 18: 12–14)

Unmerciful Servant (Matt. 18: 23–35)

Labourers in Vineyard (Matt. 20: 1–16)

Two Sons (Matt. 21: 28–31)

Marriage Feast (Matt. 22: 1–10)

Wedding Garment (Matt. 22: 11–13)

Ten Virgins (Matt. 25: 1–13)

Talents (Matt. 25: 14–30)

Sheep and Goats (Matt. 25: 31–46)

L

Physician, heal thyself (Luke 4: 23)

Two Debtors (Luke 7: 41 ff.)

Good Samaritan (Luke 10: 30–37)

Friend at Midnight (Luke 11: 5–8)

Rich Fool (Luke 12: 16–21)

Barren Figtree (Luke 13: 6–9)

Places at Table (Luke 14: 7–11)

Tower-builder (Luke 14: 28–30)

Warring King (Luke 14: 31 f.)

Lost Sheep (Luke 15: 3–7)

Lost Coin (Luke 15: 8–10)

Prodigal Son (Luke 15: 11–32)

Unjust Steward (Luke 16: 1–8)

Dives and Lazarus (Luke 16: 19–31)

Farmer and His Man (Luke 17: 7–10)

Importunate Widow (Luke 18: 1–8)

Pharisee and Publican (Luke 18: 10–14)

Pounds (Luke 19: 12–27)

* From *Interpreting the Parables* by Archibald M. Hunter. © 1960 SCM Press Limited of London. Published in the United States by Westminster Press.